Laurie Anderson

BY **JOHN HOWELL**

PHOTOGRAPHS BY *f*- STOP FITZGERALD

Thunder's
Mouth
Press

New
York

A BALLIETT & FITZGERALD BOOK

Acknowledgements
Thanks to Edit DeAk, whose tears gave me a clue to what a Laurie Anderson
performance was really about; to Janet Kardon, for a favor returned; to Liz
Barrett, for her Gadic edits; and to Laurie Anderson, whose leaps of faith are
truly inspiring. Also many thanks to Steve and Linda at Original Artists,
and Carolyn Cannon.—JH

Thanks, at Thunder's Mouth, to Neil Ortenberg for his vision and faith,
and to Anne Stillwaggon for her guidance and patience; and last, but not least,
thanks to Madeleine Morel for performing the marriage.—B&F

First edition.
First printing, 1992.

Published by Thunder's Mouth Press
54 Greene Street, Suite 4S
New York, NY 10013

Distributed by:
Publisher's Group West
4065 Hollis Street
Emeryville, CA 94608
(800)788-3123

Series editor: f-stop fitzgerald
Editorial director: Will Balliett
Line / copy editor: Elizabeth Barrett
Series book design: Frank Olinsky
Graphic artist: Beatrice Schafroth
Graphic production: Linda Rubes

Howell, John, 1947
Laurie Anderson / by John Howell: with
photographs by f-stop Fitzgerald. —1st ed.
    p.   cm.   —(American Originals)
Includes the author's interviews with Laurie Anderson.
      ISBN 1-56025-029-1 : $11.95
1. Anderson, Laurie. 1947-   . —Criticism and interpretation.
    I. Anderson, Laurie. 1947-   . II. Title.   III. Series.
              NX512.A54H6   1992
                700' .92—dc20
                92-10434 CIP

Dedication

To my three graces: Laura, Julia, and Fiona.

CONTENTS

A VOICE
FROM BEYOND

BY JOHN HOWELL

I

Several big windows in Laurie Anderson's loft in lower Manhattan face away from the city, toward the Hudson River and New Jersey—west "toward all of America," she likes to joke. At night, the view has the effect of making the country seem huge—stretching endlessly out into the darkness—and very close at the same time. The lights from across the river make New Jersey seem an arm's length away.

Night is most often the time when Anderson looks out the windows to what, as a performance artist, is her abiding subject: the politics and culture of the United States. A self-described insomniac (she even named one of her first performances *Songs and Stories for the Insomniac*), Anderson uses the driftiness of three A.M. consciousness along with the expansive, visually skewed cityscape of riverside New Jersey as a stimulus for the thoughts and sounds in her musical performances.

Laurie Anderson has won audiences in art galleries and museums, in opera houses and on pop music concert stages around the world. Sometimes called the premier performance artist of our time, Anderson prefers to call herself, "just a storyteller. What I do is just the world's oldest art form." She claims that good stories begin at home—in the early hours of the morning, when the controlling, externally driven daytime mind relaxes to allow the inner, subjective self its freedom. Many of her sing-and-tell story-songs are built around dreams, around those ordinary incidents of daily life which somehow take on a transcendent significance, and around those kinds of disconnected yet portentous thoughts that hover just below daydream level.

"As an artist, I have always tried to connect two worlds," she explains, "the so-called real world and the other world, an alternate world of possibility and chance: a dream world."

Like most New Yorkers, her life is spent mostly indoors. And like many artists, her boundaries between living and working—between life as it is lived and life as it is imagined—are blurred to produce a third possibility, a zone where the two blend in the making of art. Her loft is more than just a home; it is a nerve center for her art, the intersection of day-to-day life in Manhattan and Anderson's imagination. It is not only the place where she literally creates her art, but an inspiration for the material which makes up her performances, recordings, videos, films, and books.

"My life is hopelessly mixed up with my art and always has been," she admits. At night, she sometimes turns out the lights in her studio to allow the glow from the lights on her electronic equipment to mingle with the reflection of night lights from Newark and Jersey City across the river; their overlapping on her picture window strikes one as an illustration of her artistic approach.

Many of the actual images and sounds that recur in her works— windows and clocks, squawking birds and clicking metronomes, closing doors and honking horns—are part of her immediate environment. Speaking of the visual images in her 1989 performance piece, *Empty Places*, Anderson has said, "Every item that I see on the screen is either in my house or in a song lyric, so it's like being in this giant cartoon mock-up of my life."

Anderson has lived in lower Manhattan, just below SoHo, the contemporary art district of New York City, since 1974, when she returned from a summer vacation to find her Lower East Side apartment ransacked and several art works destroyed.

"It was a typical New York job," she says wryly. "They came in through the wall." (Typical of Anderson, she turned the incident into a story, recorded in a small book, *Light in August*.) She describes her move as "one of those obvious things: I just wanted to get closer to the scene of the action. Everybody was moving downtown." Moving closer to SoHo was a conceptual as well as a practical shift. After she graduated *magna cum laude* with a bachelor's degree in Art History from Barnard College in 1969, she earned a Master of Fine Arts degree in sculpture from Columbia University, then taught in New York's city college system for several years, and found her early inspiration and first audiences in SoHo's anything-goes seventies milieu.

SoHo was indeed overflowing with ideas and energy at that time. Art was developing myriad hybrids—conceptual art, video art, artists' books, and performance art among others. New materials and new forms appeared weekly, created by squads of new artists, fresh out of art school. The prevailing spirit among both artists and audiences was experimental, in the best sense of the word. Audiences relished the surprises offered by artists who were trying to break new ground. It was an intense, inwardly focused, clubby community, determined to separate itself from mainstream American culture at every point—from politics to art.

Anderson had been part of this world since her student days, and the move to SoHo placed her at the center of what now looks like a privileged moment in contemporary art history. From her loft, it was a walk of just a few blocks to Holly Solomon's gallery, then located downtown (it is now on Fifth Avenue); Solomon became her first art dealer. A few blocks further up the street were the Kitchen and Artists' Space, the visual and performing art centers that would sponsor her earliest exhibitions and performances. And scattered among SoHo's twenty-odd blocks were the growing numbers of galleries and cafes in which artists met and socialized.

"It was a wonderfully open time," Anderson says. "We were all pioneers. Everybody seemed to be an artist." Today, despite the changes in SoHo (the spread of trendy boutiques and the flight of many working artists) and the fact that her performances are now conducted almost exclusively in the pop entertainment and per-forming arts world rather than in alternative performance art spaces and art galleries, Anderson still exhibits personal and aesthetic traits that track back to that momentous, early seventies era.

Far from moving to more comfortable quarters as she could easi-ly have done since becoming successful, Anderson has settled even more firmly into what was once a run-down loft building. It's as if she needs to maintain a proximity to the SoHo that once nourished her, even though that community now exists more as an ideal than a reality. When she first moved into her SoHo loft, the building was in such a state of disrepair that snow lay in drifts on the floor, having blown in through broken windows. Aside from the natural impulse to create a comfortable home, Anderson's transformation of that deteriorated environment into the clean, spare space she inhabits today has a metaphorical resonance, as if to indicate that she is clearing away and simplifying her external surroundings in order to go deeper into her art.

She occupies two floors (after years of living and working on the top floor, she acquired the floor beneath her in 1990); both are immaculately but simply finished in classic modern-art spareness, with polished wood floors and bare white walls. Upstairs, fairly spartan living quarters—a functional kitchen and a bedroom only slightly larger than the bed—are at the rear of a large living area which is defined by couches grouped around a table in the middle of a large, bare space.

That relative emptiness is recent. After a kind of success peak in 1986, when she released a feature-length concert film (*Home of the Brave*), toured with a large-scale pop band, and appeared in an American Express ad, Anderson felt a need for change.

"I was tired of being 'Laurie Anderson.'" she says. "I wanted to start over. So I threw everything out of my loft. My next performance was going to be really simple, just one person—me—and a microphone." That show was called *Empty Places*, and its connection with her personal life is easy to see in the uncluttered spaciousness of her loft. The only disorder is on the table between the couches; it is piled with books, ranging from recent fiction to art catalogues and volumes on the history of science. (Laurie Anderson is, as one might surmise, a voracious reader. Merely mention an interesting book, and she will quickly whip out her notebook and write down the title and author.)

Off to one side of her living area is a small room in which her extensive archives are stored in impeccable order. Down one flight— via a spiral staircase cut into the floor—is the studio in which she does most of her recording. It looks like that of most musicians these days: stacks of electronic equipment, with hardly a musical instrument in sight. A rack of electric keyboards stands across from a computer-driven console; much of her actual composing is done with a Macintosh program. Wires lead out of the computer in all directions,

Anderson performing at a fundraiser at the Tunnel, in New York City.

and are attached to odd-looking boxes and gadgets that produce the variations of voices and sounds for which Anderson is famous.

Next to the sound studio is a rehearsal space that currently holds props and equipment for her work-in-progress. Large foam balls stand in front of a screen. They hold slide and video images, and are capable of both front- and rear-projection of those images. The visual effect is pure Anderson: a dizzying multi-dimensional, multi-layered view of simple images. On display during our visit was an extreme close-up of a plastic bunny dressed up as a prototypical French artist with beret and palette, a figure she found inside a small snow globe. "Sure looks like an artist," she says, laughing.

An adjacent room houses areas where Anderson's many collaborators work on her animated films and videos, and construct the electronic gear she needs for her performances. Standing on a table is a model of the set for *Halcion Days: Stories from the Nerve Bible*, a new live show commissioned by the World Exposition in Seville, Spain. The model resembles a small Greek temple, with large columns supporting a roof, a structure which frames a large projection screen that is off to one side. As is usual in Anderson's artistic world, things are not what they seem: the columns will emit whorling wind blasts to create a theatrical tornado out of swirling dry ice.

"I don't think anyone's done that yet on a stage," she says, as if that were all the explanation required to justify the substantial time and expense needed to generate an illusion that will fill the stage for only a few minutes. In fact, nobody has thought to do most of the things Anderson has been presenting on stages for the last twenty years. By combining age-old storytelling with futuristic, electronically produced images and sounds, telling tales and creating purely instrumental music, and appearing as Laurie Anderson examining America by talking about herself, Anderson has pioneered a kind of performance which has been variously called "electronic opera," "avant-pop music," and "multi-media performance."

She grants that performance art, "which can mean almost anything," is a tag she doesn't mind. She is not unaware that her fans often speak in breathless terms about the magic of her work, but her own commentary is often matter of fact. Many of her images and ideas are about things that are "just around." Yet her enthusiasm and downright eagerness for the flip-side, for another way of seeing, for the quirks of life, indicate that she is an artist who is attuned to a lyrical mode of translating life into art.

Touring the studio with Anderson as a guide is like being shown the latest gizmos by a prize student of Mr. Wizard—she loves to show off the latest products of her "what-if-we" thinking. As she recounts the history of her efforts to build the simulated tornado—a long tale of initial failures and mounting costs, capped by a successful conclusion—she laughs at the difficulties that have arisen from the seventies "anything goes" attitude toward art-making. If it weren't for Canal Street—the large avenue of discount hardware stores that forms the southern edge of SoHo—there might have been no visual or performance art during that decade. Not only were Canal Street's prices cheap, but the sheer variety and volume of cast-off equipment of all types gave artists ideas for new materials and new forms. Even today, many props for Anderson's shows come from those Canal Street stores. It's no accident that her company is called Canal Street Communications.

In person, Anderson comes across only occasionally as "Laurie Anderson," her performing persona. She laughs easily, seems interested in a dozen thoughts at once, and listens intently to visitors' comments. She shows off her latest works in progress with infectious enthusiasm, and takes the time to check out their effects. "How does this sound to you?" she asks, after playing a section of a new song. "Does this part sound like a closing door? What does it make you think of?"

In conversation, her voice is less deliberate, less modulated than her performing voices (of which she has several). She is almost a chain-smoker, a chronic coffee-drinker, and a no-nonsense dresser. Most of her conversations about her work and her lifestyle are presented in terms of common sense, rather than artistic abstractions. She dismisses talk of her "androgynous" appearance with a convincing, simple explanation: "Most women in the art world wear pants, don't they? They're comfortable and practical. It's not intentional, not a statement. It comes from a time when we all wore work clothes." Ditto her trademark short, spiky haircut: "You ever take care of really long hair? Takes a lot of time."

When she began to dance in her performances in the mid-eighties, after years of standing still, she explained that, too, in workaday terms: "Many of the dances began as signals to technicians—hand cues, foot cues, head cues."

At the beginning of her career she wrote art criticism, but she insists that it was an almost purely superficial exercise: "I liked meeting artists and finding out what was in their refrigerators." Her whimsy doesn't veil the seriousness behind the joke; at that time, Anderson was clearly studying how to go about being an artist. But her remarks remind us that artists also work from necessity and from materials that are at hand as much as they do from abstract conceptualization.

Equally matter of fact is her description of a trait about which she has some ambivalence: her workaholic tendency, a habit she likes to say is "just what it takes to get my work done." At the time of this interview, she was repeating this rationale somewhat wistfully. Over the years, her round-the-clock work schedule has hampered her personal life. Her close relationships have tended to be limited to collaborators. Today, in her mid-forties, she lives alone and worries about the creeping isolation that has developed during twenty years of single-minded dedication. But she also accepts it as the way of life that is necessary to produce her work.

Since she is primarily a solo performer and generates all of her own material—much of which is created by tinkering with equipment—Anderson has chosen artistic responsibilities that make lots of studio time inevitable. The gestation period for a major performance piece—encompassing songs, slides, films, props, and costumes—may stretch across years. Her periodic tours last for months and take her all over the world. Her last long tour (*Empty Places*), in 1989-90, was a stripped-down effort in comparison to its predecessor (*Natural History*), but it was still two years in the making and required a crew of seventeen and two huge trucks which carried two twenty-foot projection towers and forty-five computer-driven slide and film projectors. Since it went to many different countries (including thirty-three European cities), it was supratitled and partially spoken in ten different languages. Even a "simplified" Laurie Anderson work demands much from its creator.

She also has a habit of reworking and redoing material. Her development as an artist can be traced in a linear form only in the broadest way. Songs, stories, visual images, and other bits have often been carried over from performance to performance, and adapted for use in different media. The same song may have extra verses or a longer bridge in performance than on record; a book may record a different version altogether. This extended involvement hints at a tenacious will to wrest multiple meanings from a given piece; it also has the practical effect of increasing her workload.

In casual conversation, Anderson's talk loops around, ranges freely, almost distractedly, going back and forth as one thing leads to another. It's easy to see where one of her basic aesthetic principles—that things remind you of other things—comes from. She shares her Gemini birthday—June 5—with monologist Spalding Gray (for two of whose films, *Swimming to Cambodia* and *Monster in a Box,* she created scores), and laughs about the astrological stereotype of verbal fixation that fits both Gray and herself so well. Her stories, like Gray's, often sound like autobiographical confessions, but hers are more diffuse and symbolically loaded than are his. Sometimes her stories are deceptive as well; she has been known to adapt the stories of others and present them as the experience of the "I" who speaks in her performances.

Another consistent Anderson theme is memory. Much of her work and casual conversation begins with "I remember...." Memory is, of course, a way of retrieving time; Anderson constantly recycles her own past to create a fluid, dynamic sense of past and present.

II

"As if" is a formulation Anderson uses a lot; something is always like something else. *As:If* was also the title of her first major concert performance in 1975, at SoHo's Artists' Space, a non-profit alternative gallery that sponsored both visual art exhibitions and performances. For that performance, Anderson appeared in a white dress with her then-long hair pulled back, and adopted the guise of an ethereal storyteller, punctuating her tales with short films and tape recordings (which she projected and played on ordinary home equipment). She was intent on creating a particular ambience with complex, interactive multi-media, one that would allow access to her ideas, but would not define a specific purpose.

"As an artist I wanted to create an atmosphere that the audience could enter with a lot of images and sounds," she said. Part of that atmosphere was a free-floating message: "I leave it up to people who see my work to interpret it...I make pictures out of images and sound, and you can decide what they mean."

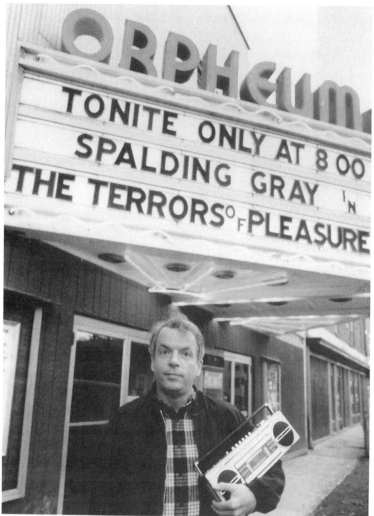

Anderson scored monologist Spalding Gray's latest film, Monster in A Box.

Audiences commonly respond to her work by saying, "She is saying what I was thinking and never said." That intimacy is the mark of a lyric method rather than an analytic one, one that allows emotional contact with an audience. Yet she has sometimes been criticized for not being more explicit in her work. To that, she says: "When people say to me, 'just say what you mean,' it seems so bizarre. If I could just say it, I would write it down on a piece of paper and stand on the street corner and hand it out. I wouldn't bother to make songs or pictures."

Her ability to engage an audience led to a rare and refreshing departure from the norm at the time: the injection of emotion into performance art. *As:If* had the audience continuously laughing, yet quietly moved; by the end of the show, the producer was in tears, reduced to saying only, "Wasn't it beautiful?" ("Beautiful" was *not* a compliment in those early performance art days.) Despite the novelty of her decidedly low-tech gadgets, Anderson clearly intended to touch her audience emotionally—and to make them laugh—an unusual goal at a time when art was fiercely conceptual and philosophically opposed to anything smacking of entertainment.

"I have always thought of my work as sensual and emotional," Anderson says. "I always wanted to have an emotional impact on my audience." Although much of the commentary on her work would pigeonhole Laurie Anderson as the "techno-wizard of electronic magic shows," she has distinguished herself from the throng of artists who work with complicated technology by using it in a context of empathetic performance. The visceral reaction of the art-world audience to *As:If* showed that her path was going to be parallel to but different from that of most performance art, which not only rarely evoked such emotional response, but actively avoided it.

As:If was her first major concert piece, but not her first public performance. In the summer of 1972, vacationing in a small Vermont town for the summer, she had produced *Automotive*, an outdoor concert for car horns.

"It was really horrible," she claims now. After *Automotive*, she performed a more emotionally laden—yet humorous—piece entitled *Duet on Ice*, in which she played violin music while wearing skates embedded in slabs of ice. "I had cold feet about performing," she says, "So I performed with blocks of ice on my feet." She also filled her violin with water so it would "weep" when she played a

Tchaikovsky concerto, punning the schmaltzy, soap opera-ish aura that the music now conjures. The performance ended when the ice melted away.

III

Laurie Anderson arrived at performing by a circuitous route. She grew up in a small suburban town near Chicago, one of eight children in her family. She learned to project her voice out of necessity: "You really had to speak up to be heard in that crowd," she says.

She remembers daydreaming often during her happy childhood: "Growing up in the Midwest left a lot to the imagination." Much of her energy went into studying the violin; she eventually played in the Chicago Youth Symphony until she gave it up at age sixteen, convinced she would never be a virtuoso player. Instead, she went to Barnard College in New York City intending to be a librarian.

"I liked to read and thought working with books was a good idea," she says. But she found herself drawn to art. After acquiring a master's degree in sculpture, she began to make sculptural objects, graphic collages, illustrated books, and super-8 films, most of them based on puns and multiple verbal allusions. Through those efforts she seemed to be working her way toward live performance.

In the mid-seventies, she became aware of the work of Vito Acconci, a poet who had begun creating performances out of his confessional obsessions. Often using his body as a material—one performance involved his apparent masturbating beneath a ramp while the audience listened to his run-on rants about sexuality—Acconci's conversion of language-based material into live events, along with his use of ordinarily hidden thoughts and feelings, were an inspiration to Anderson. They met in 1974, when he chose her work for a one-person exhibition at Artists' Space as part of its "Artists Select Artists" series. Anderson presented *O-Range*, placards which used photographs of oranges and a punning commentary to create a portrait of the world as seen through an ordinary object. Although Acconci, who always appeared as "himself" on stage, stopped performing after his confessional impulse had exhausted itself (he now creates installations), Anderson credits him with showing her the way to her own brand of work.

Throughout the seventies, she blended the basic concepts of performance art—confessional subject matter, free-form approach, and fascination with new technology—into a distinctive style. A typical work had a title with a double meaning (*For Instants, Suspended Sentences, That's Not the Way I Heard It*), was played out in a welter of mixed media (film, slides, audio tapes), and featured Anderson telling her stories from center stage. While most of the actual equipment was uncomplicated, she worked with it in ways that were far from simple. Visuals didn't merely illustrate text, music didn't merely support lyrics. The center of attention was scattered among the various media, both from sketch to sketch and from moment to moment within a particular story. She created a field of stimuli within which a viewer was free to choose a focus; constant, interactive choice was the *only* way to watch her at work.

Her most original contribution to performance art at that time was the invention of unusual gadgets, beginning with variations on her violin. She designed self-playing violins with built-in speakers. She built a tape-bow violin in which pre-recorded audio tape replaced the horsehair on the bow and a playback head replaced the strings. Moving the bow in different ways generated different voices, different sounds.

"I was just playing around, seeing what the equipment might do," she explains, noting that most of her performance tools came from tinkering rather than big ideas that technology is forced to serve.

During this time she continued to create sculptural objects for art exhibitions. One of them, *Headphone Table* (*When You We're Hear*, 1978), was exhibited at the Museum of Modern Art. Having noticed that her forearms conducted sound when she rested her elbows on a wooden table with her hands held to her head, Anderson designed a table to recreate the experience. A plain pine table concealed a recording system connected to grooves that were cut into the tabletop to seat listeners' elbows. Two different songs played at opposite ends of the table, each with physiological references: "Now You in Me Without a Body Move" and "I Remember You in My Bones." (These and other graphics, books, and sound-object sculptures would eventually be collected in a retrospective exhibition of Anderson's work at the Institute for Contemporary Art in Philadelphia in 1983, by which time she had almost ceased producing them.)

In 1976, Anderson attended *Einstein on the Beach*, a Philip Glass/Robert Wilson opera which greatly influenced her subsequent work. A four-hour meditation on the life of the great scientist, with almost continuous music accompanying lavish visual tableaux, *Einstein* gave her ideas about expanding sketchy, small-scale performance pieces to epic proportions. Her performances became bigger and longer—with more complex technology—and tackled larger subjects.

As if to confirm her new ambitions, the first of these new shows, *Americans on the Move*, appeared at a decidedly unconventional space for performance art in 1979—Carnegie Recital Hall—before it played a more typical venue, the Kitchen, later that spring. (Revised and renamed, *Americans on the Move* would eventually become Part I of *United States, I-IV*.) Nominally about an overall subject—transportation—the performance showed a new level of complexity in its interaction between spoken language and visuals; the performance tempo was faster, there were more slides and props, and more extended sequences of stories and musical interludes were strung together in an event that lasted more than ninety minutes.

Anderson also began to experiment with the voice-altering technology that would become her signature: the vocorder, a voice-activated synthesizer that divides and multiplies the voice into chords; the harmonizer, a digital processor with a range of several octaves; and the synclavier, a digital synthesizer that samples and stores sounds for playback, and makes them available for manipulated distortion. These machines gave the solo artist many voices.

"I feel a desperate need to get out of myself," Anderson admits. This new voice-altering technology allowed her to take on alternate vocal personae, most notably a deep alto that she later named "the voice of authority," an unctuous tone that is instantly identifiable as the sound of someone issuing unpleasant and coercive advice, opinions, and orders. That voice, which Anderson still uses in performances today, owed its origins to two unlikely sources, author William S. Burroughs and former president Ronald Reagan.

Anderson met Burroughs when she served as co-host for the Nova Convention, a 1978 event celebrating Burroughs with performances by Patti Smith, Philip Glass, and the B-52s, among others. Burroughs's obsession with control, his relentlessly skeptical view of power as embodied in the status quo, and his own distinctively cracked reading voice struck a chord in Anderson. It would later combine with her notion of the grandfatherly Reagan as a feel-good president to create the "voice of authority."

Anderson with some quick licks on lead violin.

The shadow of Burroughs was also evident in her next large effort, the in-progress *United States* (this section would eventually become Part II of the four-part work) staged at the Orpheum Theater in New York in the fall of 1980. The show was arranged for a proscenium theater and booked for a multi-week run (which was extended due to audience demand), marking a new level of theatrical ambition for performance art. Appearing in a black suit instead of her usual white dress or light-colored clothing, and sporting a cropped haircut formed into spikes with Vaseline, Anderson presented a dark meditation on the sorry state of the world. The visual effect was all shadows and ominous images: clocks, maps overlaid with grids, blasting rockets, towering skyscrapers, the American flag tumbling in a clothes dryer. With songs based directly on Burroughs's writings—"Let X=X," "Language Is a Virus"—and an apocalyptic attitude to match, the show was a chilling look at a bleak future. It was a turnaround from her funny, friendly performances of the past. Presented just one week before an election which everyone knew Reagan would win, its effect on audiences was hyper-emotional, especially given the cool, throwaway terms of most performance art.

Much of the entire show's appeal was captured in one song, "O Superman," a haunting ode to disembodied minds. Beginning with metronomic exhaled breaths—"hah, hah, hah, hah"—an electronically filtered voice robotically recited fragments of everyday phrases in a manner both humorous and ominous. Loaded with references to "Mom" and "petrochemical arms," the song seemed to sum up the infantile yet dangerous body politic poised to take over the country.

Typical of Anderson's work, "O Superman" had another, little-known subtext that greatly added to its impact because of her own emotional involvement with the story behind the song. She had attended a concert in which an aged tenor was attempting a comeback—and failing. In desperation, he had begun to sing Massenet's "O Souverain," a prayer for help. This accidental, inspired moment underlaid a tune that for the first time, stood alone from its performance context.

"O Superman" put Anderson on the pop culture map. Orders began to pour in for copies of the single, which had originally been produced in a pressing of one thousand for about four hundred dollars. Anderson then accepted an offer from Warner Brothers.

"I had been approached by record companies before," she says, "but I thought records were pop culture, and I was an art snob. Then there were all these orders and I couldn't fill them, so when Warner Brothers called, I signed up."

"O Superman" went to Number Two on the British pop music charts, and eventually grossed over a million dollars. (It was included on her first album for Warner Brothers, *Big Science*, which also included songs from the early parts of *United States*.)

The Warner Brothers support, both financial and logistical, gave Anderson the clout to mount her magnum opus, *United States I-IV*, as part of the Brooklyn Academy of Music's Next Wave Festival. A performance event with outsize numbers—it lasted over seven hours, took place on two separate nights, included some seventy-eight segments of both new and recycled songs and stories, and involved eleven other performers as well as Anderson on stage—*United States* signaled Anderson's ambition to produce a radically revised notion of contemporary grand opera.

Her goal was nothing less than "a performance portrait of the country." Each of the parts had a nominal theme—"Transportation," "Politics," "Money," and "Love"—but the distinctions between them were not hard and fast. Its recurrent themes in both language and images were taken from the American vernacular: the road, the dream-like quality of ordinary life, the impact of media on modern culture. It included moments that recalled her background in sculpture and visual art—notably a percussion solo played on her amplified skull—but was made up principally of skits built around combinations of slide projections and film, coupled with stories and songs.

A virtual anthology of her performances to date, *United States* rapidly escaped the confines of avant-garde performance art and was seen as the cutting edge of contemporary performance, period. It was captured on a four-record set, documented in a mass-distribution book of the same title (Harper & Row), and traveled on a worldwide tour playing large concert halls and opera houses.

Anderson next set out on a new, pop-inflected phase of her career. She assembled *Mister Heartbreak*, an album of unrecorded material from *United States* and some new songs, with an ensemble of "progressive" professional musicians (Peter Gabriel, Nile Rodgers, Adrian Belew). She also created a music video for the album's selected single, "Sharkey's Day," a catchy, Burroughs-inspired tune with state-of-the-art production quality. Other songs were inspired by literary influences as diverse as Thomas Pynchon, "Gravity's Angel," and Shakespeare, "Blue Lagoon."

She installed a fully equipped studio in her loft and embarked on a lengthy tour. In 1986, a new, more densely musical version of her work formed the core of *Home of the Brave*, a concert documentary film. Coincidentally with the movie's release, she began another domestic tour, *Natural History*, again with a big band. All of this activity brought her large, new audiences and increased pop notoriety.

But criticism from the art world mounted with her new pop visibility. From her remarks at the time, it seems clear that Anderson was stung by comments that accused her of betraying her fine arts origins.

"The avant-garde gave up on me," she said. "At first, it hurt my feelings, but then I realized that's what an avant-garde does: protect itself. As soon as I began to talk to people on the outside, I could no longer be considered part of that group."

Audiences and critics seemed disappointed that *Home of the Brave* was a concert film instead of an ingenious Anderson concoction, and despite its many *echt*-Anderson moments, it remained somewhat inert, more of a document than a performance.

"I should never have directed it," Anderson now says. "It was too much to be in every scene and stage everything at the same time. I also think my next film will be a primary experience, not a secondary one," referring to the unsatisfactory documentary mode of *Home of the Brave*.

In another mood, though, Anderson wonders if there was such a thing as an avant-garde. "I think that I'm an avant-garde artist because I still want to rattle people's expectations. But I don't know what that word means anymore, really. Who knows if there is an avant-garde? It won't really disappear, I guess. There are plenty of rules left, just waiting to be broken and I'll do my part."

Today, she prefers to sidestep the whole debate. "I don't think of my work as avant-garde," she says. "I'm just a storyteller." That simpler view of herself was evident in her major performance work, *Empty Places*, which returned to a solo format. Even though the technology for the show was more complex than any of Anderson's previous works—for the first time she used a visual computer to control and drive her images—*Empty Places* featured her alone on stage, telling tales and singing songs. As if to rebut charges that her work had become overly concerned with the technology that powered it, *Empty Places* became something more of a polemic than previous work had been.

"I wanted it to feel more raw, more jagged than my past work," she said. "It's an unadorned story about pain. I'm angrier now than I was." Her anger stemmed from what she saw as the legacy of social devastation stemming from the Reagan era.

"It's about how much the world has changed in the last few years," she said in 1989, when the work debuted. "More than anything, *Empty Places* is about suffering; there's no point in being clever or double-edged about suffering."

Like a modern-day Weegee, Anderson stalked the city by night, shooting thousands of slides and dozens of films of the decrepit warehouses, abandoned buildings, and empty parking lots that gave *Empty Places* its dark tone. But she avoided taking photographs of people, even though she stepped over increasing numbers of the homeless on her own doorstep. "It was too painful," she said. Her intent was a direct exposé of the wrecked material and spiritual state of the country.

"I wanted to write a poster," she explained. "I had always said 'I'll present a picture and you make up your mind about what it means.' Then I thought, 'I know what I think about what's going on and I'm going to say it.'"

Another element in her more straightforward performance was a major change for her: she began singing. After years of singsong talk in her songs, Anderson began to seriously study voice and developed a soprano that had unexpected consequences. It changed her approach somewhat.

"It's very vulnerable to sing. It's hard to sing things that are severely ironic. Slightly ironic, yes, but severely ironic, no. It's too hard. So now that I had this different voice I started writing about really different things, from a more female point of view."

Empty Places premiered at the Spoleto Festival in Charleston, South Carolina, and appeared in the Brooklyn Academy of Music's Next Wave Festival. It eventually played in 133 cities in the United States and Europe, and toured parts of South America as well. Its combination of a no-nonsense Anderson, a complex yet unobtrusive technology, and a more direct message struck a chord with all kinds

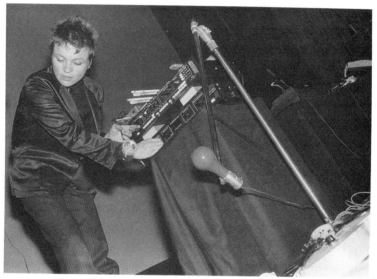

Trademark Anderson staging (red lightbulb in front of her and white violin on the floor in foreground), at the Market Street Cinema, San Francisco.

of audiences, and did much to recover her reputation as an artist with something serious to say.

Empty Places was followed by an even starker, bare-bones performance, *Voices from the Beyond*. A nearly two-hour monologue, with merely two or three songs and only one visual image to punctuate her talking—a slide of a road disappearing in the distance—the piece highlighted her central tenet that she is first a storyteller and offered an even greater tilt toward unabashed content than did *Empty Places*.

"It's a reaction to the Gulf War," she said. (The war had broken out as she was developing the monologue.) An extension of the pointed messages presented in *Empty Places*, *Voices from the Beyond* featured Anderson in the guise of an acerbic Mark Twain, as opposed to her more genial Will Rogers-type persona. Her targets included censorship in the arts, the second-class citizenship of women, and the know-nothing patriotism that she feels encouraged the war in the Middle East. Her political punditry was interspersed with some of her usual stock-in-trade: personal anecdotes, travel vignettes, and childhood dreams. But the material was all put in the service of the larger subject of freedom and control.

Spoken in cool tones, Anderson's unvarnished polemic was a bleak coda to the complex *United States I-IV*. *Voices from the Beyond* also had a provisional nature that seemed to free Anderson artistically; no longer did everything have to be just-so for the notorious perfectionist. She read much of the performance from a notebook, changed its content from time to time depending on the news of the moment, and presented a persona more like her actual self, which lent an enhanced emotional impact to the work.

IV

At mid-career Laurie Anderson is still evolving. A new performance, *Halcion Days: Stories from the Nerve Bible*, debuted last spring in Seville as part of the World Exposition, and is scheduled to tour this year and next. A solo performance again with major high-tech support, it contains stories and songs in her usual sketch-anthology format, continuing with the political concerns of *Voices from the Beyond* in a multi-media mode much like that of *Empty Places*.

A new album is also in the works, a suite of songs recorded in the studio for a change, before they were ever performed live. (Most of her other albums have been recorded after and/or concurrent with a show.) And research is underway for a massive book that will document her entire career in a lavish visual presentation. Beyond that?

"Well, deadlines always motivate me," she says, falling back on one of her disarming, matter-of-fact explanations. "I'll see what's going on when I get my next commission."

Like any true performance artist, Anderson will derive her cues for the future from an immediate context. By focusing on the process of discovery, Laurie Anderson maintains a palpable connection between life and work that keeps her performance truly alive.

"I used to make these five-year plans," she says, laughing, "but now I'm going along for the ride, just like everyone else." Mutual openness is what excites Anderson and her audiences. For her, success is a shared plunge into the unknown.

"Sometimes people tell me 'Oh, I got so many ideas from your work.' Then they tell me what the ideas were, and they have nothing whatsoever to do with what I said or did. This tells me that the work was really a success—when other people take it and use it in a way I'd never dreamed of."

ARTIST
IN DIALOGUE

JOHN HOWELL: When you begin a show, you have two things going on: first of all, you've contracted to do a show.

LAURIE ANDERSON: That's the first thing. The second thing is, I try to get out of the contract. The third thing is, my manager says, "You have to pay them a lot of money to get out of the contract." And I say, "Oh my God, did I sign that?" and she says, "Yes, you did," then I kick and scream for a while and I'm sure it's going to be the largest humiliation in my life. This show is no exception; I'm in that panic period right now.

HOWELL: They all start out that way?

ANDERSON: And some finish out that way, too. Well, not really. It's never as bad as I think.

HOWELL: How do you start?

ANDERSON: Most of the early stuff gets thrown away. I started this time by animating Barbie dolls, because of the Anita Hill hearings, probably. I wanted to make a bimbo say something other than you'd expect, and Barbie being the biggest bimbo of all, I thought it'd be fun.

HOWELL: Did you know that they make "natural" Barbie now? Smaller breasts. I saw my first one last week. I really had to look closely to see the difference.

ANDERSON: It's subtle. It's one size smaller or bigger. I have a Barbie, a black Barbie, an MC Hammer, and a Ken doll. I animated them all. There they are, just talking, and I put them in the computer and did this elaborate thing with them. But also I learned a lot about the animation program, so it was a way of gearing up for the show.

HOWELL: Did you have a general concept for the show and you thought this would go along well with it, or did you just have the Anita Hill thing on your mind and start building from there?

ANDERSON: I have a series of ideas, but they're very general.

HOWELL: What are some of those general ideas?

ANDERSON: Hmmm...Kurt Vonnegut, time going backwards—I like that a lot.

HOWELL: I once asked how you define performance art and you thought the great thing about it was that you couldn't define it. People think of a performance artist in many ways: as a confessional or autobiographical person, as a shaman receiving messages from the *Zeitgeist*, as someone who brings things from home to show them to other people. What does it mean to you?

ANDERSON: You've summed it up. I was on "Crossfire" [*a public television talk show—JH*] to discuss the NEA [National Endowment of the Arts] situation, debating with David Horowitz—he used to be a leftie, now he's a rightie. Naturally this question came up: "So, Miss Anderson, what is performance art?" And I said exactly what you just did. It's that whole combination. But I added that the corn-for-porn discussion in Congress could qualify [as performance art], because there's a certain amount of absurdity in it and a certain amount of messing around with language. So, our side won the "Crossfire" debate, only because Horowitz said things like: "Now, Miss Anderson, I understand, I mean, I'm a big fan of yours, and I know the well-heeled patrons who come to your shows." He was digging himself in further and further and I was trying to look noncommittal, and he said, "Someone like you would never have gotten a National Endowment of the Arts grant, right?" I've gotten so many NEA grants—several individual ones and a bunch that were hidden,

> *People think of performance art like the New York Post describes it: gay black men with holes cut in the backs of their pants or some person smearing chocolate on herself.*

you know, you go to a university or a theater and it's sponsored by the National Endowment in some way.

HOWELL: Do you think, in the public mind, performance art translates as something salacious?

ANDERSON: Yes, yes. Now it is just like what the *New York Post* says in its editorials—gay black men with holes cut in the backs of their pants. Just like the Pat Buchanan campaign spots. Or some person smearing chocolate on herself. That's what it is for everybody. That's what was so annoying about doing this "Crossfire" debate. The Endowment has done a million projects in twenty-six years; ten of those have been controversial. That means nine hundred thousand, nine hundred and ninety projects were successes. Just think about it. That's an excellent rate.

HOWELL: You do shows with music and visuals; I suppose that by salacious performance art standards they're pretty—

ANDERSON: —tame.

HOWELL: I mean, you don't do anything—

ANDERSON: I've never taken my clothes off.

HOWELL: So do people try to separate you from performance art? Do they say, "Well, you're really a musician; you're really a filmmaker."

ANDERSON: Yeah, well, I could hide over in any corner I wanted to. It's very handy. And also it's more entertaining for me. If I just can't stand looking at another goldfish in the video animation that I'm doing, I just make an audio tape. Or I can spend fourteen hours in a row, trying to track down technological problems.

HOWELL: I remember, when it started, "performance" was simply an adjective in front of the word "artist" to describe somebody who did something live.

ANDERSON: Yeah, that's all it really is. Something live that doesn't look too much like theater. That's all you can say about it. Other than that, you just can't say anything coherent.

HOWELL: Because so many of your stories seem autobiographical, people often assume that performance artists are presenting themselves.

ANDERSON: Every word is true!

HOWELL: What does that mean? When you're onstage, obviously you're performing. I think one of the assumptions about performance art is that you're bringing more of what you really might be—whatever that is—than an actor who's asked to play a specific role. Yes? No?

ANDERSON: Sure. But then, about ten years ago I discovered the second person and I realized I could say "you" instead of "me," and that changed everything. I didn't have to stick to "me." It wasn't like I was giving anyone advice—God forbid—but I had learned an informal kind of address and it made a lot of sense to me. And I tried some "he" things too, and some "she" things. "They" is too divisive.

HOWELL: Why's that?

ANDERSON: Because it's "us" and "them." I love that bathroom piece where an artist just changed the men's and women's room to "us" and "them," and nobody knew which one to go into. Who are "they?" "They" are the enemy, usually.

HOWELL: Well, many of your shows were solo, and the stories began with something like, "When I was in Alaska last summer..." There was a dialogue, but there wasn't another performer. Did you have to fight a pressure to make that, "It's me here by myself, and all of you?"

ANDERSON: No, when I used "you," it was singular. It really was. And I didn't try to do if-I-were-you things because I could never imagine that. When people say that to me my eyes cross. If you were *me*? I mean, if every single molecule of your body changed into ones that looked exactly like mine and you had all of my memories and every hair follicle? I couldn't imagine it, so there was always a strict division between "me" and "you." That's why I single people out in performances. They know it, too. They write to me: "I know you were looking at me." It may not have been that person exactly, but I was looking at someone and talking right to them.

HOWELL: You studied art history at Barnard, but I haven't heard you on the part where they didn't mention women in the art history books?

ANDERSON: Yeah, because it was a women's college and we were the brave new women of the future.

HOWELL: Did that schooling actually help you?

ANDERSON: It did. I chose to do that because I thought that I could express myself better. I hadn't ever had a chance to do that. I went to a regular high school. And I really wanted to see what that was like to be in a situation like that [*Barnard, a women's college—JH*]. I'm really glad that I did, because it was very supportive.

HOWELL: Was that something that stayed with you through your work?

ANDERSON: Yes.

Anderson as a "non-mathematician", discussed some numbers that had been bothering her (from Home of the Brave).

HOWELL: Are there specific things you got out of it, that have influenced your work one way or another?

ANDERSON: Just watching Barbara Novak [*head of the art department at Barnard at that time—JH*] on the phone. I would go into her office and think, "I'm in the office of the President of the United States." She was on the phone with Andy Warhol, then she'd hang up and Bob Smithson would call, and I thought, "Real artists! And she's talking to them on the phone!" I thought she was tied in to the center of the world. And then *Artforum* would call her—that's how I started writing. She's a really exciting person. We would have these wild seminars, really wild debates. It was great. I actually think it's a really good thing. Well, it was a really good thing for me; I'm not sure it's really good for other people. I know the statistics on women's colleges and that women tend to be a little more aggressive if they have that experience, a little more confident. I do remember noticing, in the courses that I took at Columbia, that when there were men in the classes, they were definitely favored. And I really, *really* didn't enjoy that. And also, I graduated in 1969, when it was still a little bit unusual for a woman to have a career. We were still definitely passed over in favor of the men.

HOWELL: Do you teach now?

ANDERSON: No.

HOWELL: Have you thought about it?

ANDERSON: This last tour [*Voices from the Beyond*] felt enough like that. Although, you know, the last talk I gave before I decided to wrap it up was at Harvard and it was fun, mostly because the students were wonderful. They were just like shining lights. Each one totally different. And I got to meet some of them. I did the talk in the theater, presented as a kind of concert. Then I met with students, and that was really fascinating. I also met with this group called the Nieman Fellows; it's a wonderful program for journalists. I met with them one morning, and it was one of the best mornings I've ever had. All these people from all over the world get to spend a year at Harvard studying whatever they want. The most enlightened thing about the program is that their spouses also have the privilege of attending anything and learning anything. They do that because the kind of thing that destroys those residencies is the spouses going, "We're going where? To do what? For a year?

You're going to take off for a year?" But with the Nieman program, you go, "So are you. Whatever you want to learn." And they pay you. These people were the most awake group of people I've ever been in a room with. They were so in touch with things and had so many questions and so many opinions. It was really fascinating. You couldn't get away with anything.

HOWELL: They're smart people.

ANDERSON: Not just smart but happy. Happy to learn things. Happy to be wrong if they were wrong. Happy to be right if they were right. They were just generally curious.

HOWELL: They're in that ideal zone where it's not driven toward a particular purpose.

ANDERSON: It's just to find out things. And there were no personal grudges. It was just, "That's a good point. I hadn't thought of it that way." It wasn't protective. It was people who really wanted to change and learn. That's so rare. So many people are protecting their turf—they have to be right, because their whole world will be destroyed if one little thing is chipped at.

HOWELL: When did you first decide to do performance art?

ANDERSON: I had done some kind of very big thing at Lewisohn Stadium up at City College, arranging oranges in this huge stadium and taking photographs at various points of view and making up stories about distance and memory. I remember thinking, "Why am I doing this?" I was just deciding whether I would be an artist. I didn't make that decision until I'd spent several months in bed.

> *I didn't decide to be an artist until I had spent several months in bed. I didn't want to get up until I had something I really, really wanted to do.*

It was 1972. I was teaching at night, so I could stay in bed until two or three or four in the afternoon. And I decided I needed a plan; I didn't want to get out of bed until I had something I really, really, *really* wanted to do. Not something I had to do. I was teaching at Staten Island Community College, City College, and Pace. These were mostly people getting their degree at night or on Sunday morning. A lot of them were Turkish cab drivers or something like that, looking for an easy course that would get them the credit.

HOWELL: Sunday morning art looked good.

ANDERSON: At City College, though, some of them were really brilliant but they couldn't read. I especially remember one particular guy; I was showing this slide of a Goya nude and he looked at it and said, "Could I talk to you after class?" and I said "Okay, fine." What he wanted was her phone number, and I said, "Look, if she ever existed—which we're not really sure—she's dead now. She does not have a phone." Then I said, "I'm going to take you to the museum—just you and me—and I'll show you what this is." And we went and took pictures of them, took him to the lab, showed him how this was done, that these were old pictures. And at the end of this three-day thing, he still wanted her phone number, so I gave up. (Laughs.) Then he started to show up at my place on East Second Street. He'd call me up and say, "I'm right downstairs," and I'd look out my window and he was down there wanting to talk—wanting her phone number and wanting to talk.

HOWELL: Was this your first introduction to the kind of passion art can arouse?

ANDERSON: I had seen that before, actually. There was a lecturer at Barnard who would show pictures of still lifes and she'd go up and start stroking the fruit on the screen or something like that. We all got pretty excited.

HOWELL: She was kind of irreverent.

ANDERSON: Yeah, she really was. (Laughs.)

HOWELL: You went from oranges in the stadium to performing?

ANDERSON: Well, that wasn't the way I hooked into performing at all. It was teaching more than anything else, telling those stories to my class. It takes a lot to turn Sunday morning at Pace University into other-worldly experience. But if you really don't go by the book, if you just make stuff up, it's so much more fun. Those people really didn't care whether I was telling them the truth or not.

HOWELL: Are you telling us that you made up your own version of art history?

ANDERSON: Completely. That lecturer at Barnard stroking her peaches was not that different. Well, it was different because the stories I made up had nothing to do with anything I'd ever read in art history books.

HOWELL: You had the frame of art history to play against. How did you end up doing your first show at Artists' Space? Had you been performing before that?

ANDERSON: In 1972, I did a concert in Rochester. I went to this town and saw that it was so demeaning. They were giving a little concert in a gazebo and people who came would not even get out of their cars. And I thought, "You should definitely have a car concert in a place like that." So I wrote this thing for car horns and tried to audition people, but nobody—I mean *nobody*—in Rochester wanted to be a part of it until I made it competitive. I set up a thing in the Grand Union parking lot saying: "Does your car hit a C-sharp?" Then people thought, "I wonder if it does." It was like an audition. I'd say, "No, your car doesn't hit that note, sorry." And they'd say, "Well, can I be in it anyway?" (Laughs.) So we did this thing, and it just sounded like a bunch of barking seals. It really was pretty bad. I did it with iridescent guidebooks with color coded scores, and you just honked every time I put my hand over red. Red-red-blue-yellow; it sounded really strange, but it was a lot of fun. At that time I was also doing my *Institutional Dream Series*, which came from falling asleep in art history class. I would drift off and have dreams that mixed my personal life with art history. I'd get them very deeply confused, so I did this whole *Institutional Dream Series*. I'd go to different places, like night court, or a boat that was docked in the South Street Seaport, or a women's bathroom, or the library at Columbia University and fall asleep. I'd write down these dreams, you know, whether they had any association with that institution and how those things can seep in. It was pretty interesting. Especially the night court. That was kind of like looking at a photo story.

HOWELL: Which was a very pervasive conceptual art thing at the time. It did have a strong performance idea to it.

ANDERSON: A lot of these things were about how to be vulnerable in a bureaucratic situation.

HOWELL: How to wake up by falling asleep.

ANDERSON: Yes. The first time I did it, [*fell asleep in a public place—JH*], there were all these cleaning women in the bathroom and they got very angry that I was sleeping there. It was such a taboo to them, that someone could lose consciousness like that in public. They got very upset and started hitting me with their brooms to wake me up. And I'm like a narcoleptic. (Laughs.) I could sleep anywhere for a brief period of time. In the *Institutional Dream*

Anderson deep in concentration, performing United States I-IV at the Kabuki Theater in San Francisco.

Series, I also used photographs I'd taken while I was walking alone on East Houston Street. Guys would go, "Hey, baby" or make some comment more elaborate than that, and I would take their picture. I got interested in that and in the range of their reactions when I'd say, "Do you mind if I take your picture?" Some people saw it as aggression. Some guys just totally flipped it around and were flattered. "Me? Really! How great. Thanks." And it became a much more human sort of experience.

HOWELL: Were you thinking of it as art?

ANDERSON: Oh, absolutely. This was the early seventies, so there was some kind of a political tinge. That work was always about how to relate to the institution. So much of the sixties was about "We're going to bring the big boys down," or "We're going to write songs about who's actually in power and we're going to expose it." In fact, it just didn't work that way. Even in the early seventies, you knew it wasn't going to work that way.

HOWELL: Well, there was some idea that you could rattle their cage with art that had to do with social behavior. But you didn't quite know what was going to happen.

ANDERSON: No, you didn't. But I didn't have a lot of faith in direct political action.

HOWELL: Artists' Space was supposed to be an alternative way to get famous artists—at least ones who were well-known—to pick unknown ones, thinking that would help draw some attention to them. It was kind of democratic; anybody could put their slides on display there. I think people got very jaded about things like that in the eighties. Everything was evaluated in terms of status and money. But I remember after that first show of yours, I was interested in how someone moved from visual into performance art. What made you want to do that? You've already described one thing, the teaching, but I remember you saying you loved audiences.

ANDERSON: Well, I liked that, but I was doing a lot of writing, too. I wrote a series of short stories with illustrations which looked a lot like the slides I used in *As: If.* Words and water were the ideas. There were two words on a slide, with a colon between them. There was always some connection between language and water, so all the stories had some kind of water in them. The slides were like big books to me. They weren't supposed to be movies. The movies would be crossword puzzles, animated crossword puzzles.

HOWELL: In that performance, *As:If,* you used the song "Splish Splash, I Was Taking a Bath," but I don't remember what went with it.

ANDERSON: Some kind of baptism thing, I think. It was called autobiographical art, and this really was. It was about my religious upbringing. I was obsessed with making the stories *not* very interesting; I wanted to simply remember exactly what happened. Once I said it, though, it was another story. Just the telling of it makes it completely different, so I never really said anything that I felt truly represented what had actually happened. Never. I would only remember one aspect. There had been ten things happening, but the mind patterns things and arranges them so that the only thing you see is some kind of thread.

HOWELL: Was it as cynical as Twain saying, "Never let the truth get in the way of a good story?"

ANDERSON: I really didn't think that I was telling true stories. I was trying to understand how memory worked, and that was one of the reasons I decided not to document any of that stuff—which I'm really sorry about now. I thought, "I want to just exist in people's memories and then when they forget, that's it."

HOWELL: Were you surprised that people found the stories funny or moving?

ANDERSON: I was. I thought they were just very mundane sort of incidents and that I was structuring them around certain ideas.

HOWELL: At this time, it was still kind of weird to hear people laugh at those kind of performances. Ordinarily, people would watch very quietly. But Artists' Space was decidedly funkier than other galleries. People laughed when they thought the performance was funny.

ANDERSON: I remember being kind of self-conscious because I was wearing a stupid dress. I remember thinking it was a really good idea, then when I got in front of the audience wearing that thing, I thought, "I'm in my pajamas—this is my worst nightmare." (Laughs.) And Bob [*Bielicki, technical advisor—JH*] had designed a kind of belt that I wore under my arms; it had a microphone sticking out, because I had to play the violin and talk into the microphone at the same time. And I was wearing the skates. It took me a long time to get through all of the people on the floor to the stage, and I remember thinking, "I'm about to really humiliate myself in front of my friends."

HOWELL: But you got used to performing live?

ANDERSON: I actually found that I enjoyed it. Once I got over feeling like I was a real fool, I thought, "It's not that bad to be a fool. What do I want to be? Sophisticated? Intelligent? I'd much rather be a fool." It was really surprising that the audience responded, too.

HOWELL: I remember people laughing, I remember some pretty strong reactions.

ANDERSON: And that part was really quite surprising to me. I had not written it as this-is-going-to-be-funny. And it's the same thing now; I write something and I'm not sure what's funny and what isn't, until I see what people's reactions are.

HOWELL: I remember saying to you that it was a very Gemini performance.

ANDERSON: That's right. There were always two things happening.

HOWELL: Dialectics.

ANDERSON: I used a tape recorder to do a fake tape-delay. I mean, everything was so phony, it's ridiculous. It was pretty schizophrenic, as all my work has been. We Geminis naturally concede both sides of the story.

HOWELL: Geminis are also supposed to have a psychology called apperception, the quality of watching yourself do something while you're doing it. It's also called sociopathic dissociation or some other hideous thing. Geminis are supposedly very verbal which removes you from the thing. You're very aware of "Here's the language, here's the object."

ANDERSON: That has always been my defense. That removal and so much language going on. I'm going to do a theater thing in Spain and Germany, and I'm trying to do the scariest thing—just going with no props. It's so frightening to me. It wouldn't be, if there weren't all these expectations that people have of me.

HOWELL: They think you're a one-person opera. You travel with trucks.

ANDERSON: Right. Well, I have to bring a couple of things because it's so frightening otherwise.

HOWELL: I would say another thing about language: people who use it have a strong relation to it. It is abstract, but it's also very tactile. Certain words look good, others don't. You really have strong visceral reactions to phrases.

ANDERSON: That's why doing something in foreign languages is so scary. If you're trying to describe something like "withered magazines," it won't do anything unless you get the exact right word for "withered."

HOWELL: One of my favorite stories is about you learning Japanese from someone with a speech impediment.

ANDERSON: That was terrifying. (Laughs.) He was so polite about it, too.

HOWELL: During the mid-seventies, your format stayed the same, but you got bigger and more sophisticated. You actually didn't have to run all of it yourself.

ANDERSON: For about three or four years—between 1975 and 1978—I was doing lots of small tours. I went up to Buffalo, and did a piece called *Like a Stream*, and I did some things in DC Space that were just for that evening. I thought, "I can never repeat any of these things." That was my policy; I did a lot of stuff like that. Then I realized I needed [some of those stories for other pieces], and I started doing more of that. I still do.

HOWELL: That makes sense, because in your work things are constantly evolving back and forth between language and objects. It seems organic to your work to have it be vignette, vignette, vignette...I remember a performance at Holly Solomon's that was a one-night preview of one of your shows. It may have been the year before the Orpheum, when they were starting to get big-scale.

ANDERSON: The Orpheum was the biggest scale show I'd done to that point [1980]. It might not have been the biggest place, but it was the most worked-out version. That was the first two parts of *United States*. Or maybe it was just *Part II*, I'm not sure now.

HOWELL: I think what was most striking about the Orpheum was that suddenly it was not just in little art spaces with their limitations and arbitrariness. It was onstage; it was like seeing your work in a theater—very bizarre. And that particular performance was on the eve of the Reagan era. I remember such a feeling of dread, that whatever had happened in the sixties and seventies, this was going to be more awful.

ANDERSON: What I remember was having to change one of the stories from "I dreamed I was Jimmy Carter's lover" to "I dreamed I was Ronald Reagan's lover." (Laughs.)

HOWELL: Since it was right on the eve of the election. There was a special emotion about it because of the dread.

ANDERSON: I appreciate these moments of dread.

HOWELL: I think "O Superman" had an appeal that was not just as a

Lady Liberty looms in the background, as a dual drum set almost dwarfs Anderson in the left foreground.

piece of music.

ANDERSON: It was the moment.

HOWELL: It locked into the prevalent mood of return-to-Mommy, I wish Mommy would get us out of this hideous fix. We were sixties kids and we didn't think it was going to be like this when we grew up. "Here come the planes" seemed to be appealing to a higher authority of some sort.

ANDERSON: Yeah, and then suddenly realizing that Mom is not that cozy.

HOWELL: Yeah. She's electronic. That was the first time you'd gone out of art spaces to perform. Suddenly you were on pop charts, suddenly there was a whole other awareness and appreciation for what you were doing.

ANDERSON: Thinking back on it, I appreciate it, but I see all the things that were negative about it as well. It's only recently that I've thought about it in that way, looking through these pictures from the almost-minstrel era, when I was wearing these glossy white suits and doing showman, very eighties stuff.

HOWELL: Maybe showmanship was a way to let more people see what you were doing.

ANDERSON: Yeah, and it was the strangest thing to record, too, because in a lot of ways it was quite showoffish.

HOWELL: You're still unhappy with it?

ANDERSON: I never really liked it. I was really uncomfortable with all those people prancing around. I was kind of embarrassed by it. I think of it now as a time when I had gotten deep into the fallout of the media thing; I was beginning to be seen as a sort of pop culture person. You know, "It's not just provoking, but *entertaining*." It was not a happy time for me.

HOWELL: Was that because after the Orpheum there was still all that momentum which carried you into *United States*?

ANDERSON: I didn't finish that until 1983, when I presented all four things.

HOWELL: But that was sort of a culmination of what you had started—and were still doing—even though the pop scene was still happening around you.

ANDERSON: It was 1978 to 1983. In 1984 I wanted to get to another record right away, so I did *Mr. Heartbreak*, which I have a feeling is one of my favorite records. But then again, I haven't heard it since I made it, so I am not a good judge of this stuff at all.

HOWELL: Well, *United States* was colossal. I mean, what would you expect from someone who had been going to twelve-hour Philip Glass concerts and fourteen-hour Robert Wilson operas, and who wouldn't bury any of her good stories? (Laughs.) *Mr. Heartbreak* felt like a relief.

ANDERSON: It was a vacation for me.

HOWELL: It also felt like you were playing with the pop stuff a little bit. It had some music that anybody could easily grab onto. And it had a sort of delight in it.

ANDERSON: Right. My new studio was working and I spent a lot of time looking out at the river, and I thought, "This is delightful." I just wanted to write some idling music from Manhattan.

HOWELL: That makes sense, because not only was *United States* big, it was heavy. It was politics, anger, dread, and all those wonderful feelings that we all had at the same time. *Mr. Heartbreak* let us just enjoy the moment. I think it would make you happy if you played it today.

I never, ever listen to my old stuff. If I do a radio show and they want to play it, I bring ear plugs. I cannot bear it.

ANDERSON: I wouldn't have the nerve. (Laughs.)

HOWELL: Do you ever listen to your old stuff?

ANDERSON: I never, ever do. And when I have to do radio shows and they say, "Let's listen to some of your old albums," I bring ear plugs. I cannot bear it.

HOWELL: There was the feeling that the performance at the Orpheum did one step, and then "O Superman" kind of brought you to pop, and the momentum carried you to *United States*. So that was the culmination of both the art audience that you had dragged along with you and the new audience that had been attracted because they said, "What's this?" There was a kind of wild mixture of those audiences.

ANDERSON: Yeah, there was.

HOWELL: What do you think about *United States* now?

ANDERSON: I'm struck by how personal it is, actually. I mean, at the time I was thinking about it as having these big topics, but a lot of the stories were about "My sister and I used to play this game called Red Hot..." (Laughs.) And you're thinking, "What does that have to do with anything?" A lot of it was like that. It was a good title. And, of course, there were a lot of political things.

HOWELL: There were four themes. Transportation—

ANDERSON: Politics, money, and love.

HOWELL: A lot of things came under those. I guess the song "Blue Lagoon" came under "Love," but it didn't really matter. Those themes were just handles to help guide the audience through the performance. Did you feel that people wanted it to be more political than it was?

ANDERSON: I think people's perception was that it was more political than it actually was, because of the title and those subtitles. Maybe a third of it was quite political, but the rest was totally personal, just anecdotes. It's about the same kind of mixture of stuff that's in the talks I've been doing during the last year. It's somewhat political and then there's some stuff that's not even translated into songs or anything like that. It's just straight: "This is happening, look at it from a slightly different angle." I remember being terrified I would run out of stories. I always wondered what Spalding [*Gray, the monologist—JH*] would do when he ran out.

HOWELL: Spalding told me once he initially had that fear and then he realized that as long as he was alive, things would happen. The trick was not to get locked into a formula about what the story should be so that he would start looking for them before he had lived them.

ANDERSON: It's really true. Just try to do as many disparate things as possible.

HOWELL: Spalding has been accused of things like buying a house so he could have a story for a performance, but he said that there were a lot of less drastic things that he could have done, he really didn't have to buy *a* house. What audiences don't see are the things that don't turn into stories. I remember he went to Washington for some time and lived there—

ANDERSON: —I remember that. He was trying to be Mr. Smith.

HOWELL: He said, "Ah, it didn't work." Nobody sees the parts that don't work.

ANDERSON: That's what's wrong with a plot; it takes all of the boring days out. I don't really need a lot of big themes. I really enjoy small events, so most of the stuff that I do doesn't have a plot. It has a structure, but it doesn't have a plot.

HOWELL: At one point you said you'd never make a film again. Was it the kind of film that *Home of the Brave* was that bothered you?

ANDERSON: Yeah, it was just looking at my face. And honestly, I should never, ever have done that. I directed it, then sat there for almost a year cutting it and mixing it. By the time it came out, it ran maybe three or four days on Fifty-Seventh Street before it closed. That was devastating. It was *really* devastating reading the review; I remember Roma [*Baran, the producer—JH*] and I sitting in a cab—we'd just spent a year-and-a-half on this thing—and the review just said, "Blah blah blah blah...You can skip this one." (Laughs.) We were speechless. Not that I was shocked by the response; you could easily have said awful, awful, awful things about it—much more awful than that review. But still, it was a dismissal. And I thought, in a way, "Well, thank God," because if I had written a review of that movie, it would have been: "People prancing around showing off. This is disgusting!"

HOWELL: You were already preparing for the worst.

ANDERSON: Yeah, but hoping for, "Great! What a delight! All these colors! All this action! How exciting! Nobody's ever done this before! Look at those Oskar Schlemmer design things!" (Laughs.)

HOWELL: But inevitably in the career of any performing artist something like that happens.

ANDERSON: Of course.

HOWELL: How many ego-deaths can you suffer? If you're a performer, a lot. Most people do it quietly; performers do it onstage. But the cassette of that movie has a life, because there are many people who have never seen you live—they have heard your music and they want to see what it looks like. They take it as a documentary film of a concert, and they watch it with interest.

ANDERSON: That's nice. (Laughs.) I think I'm quite over this but I do remember just dying. It was just the worst.

HOWELL: Earlier, you said you originally never wanted to record anything, that you only wanted it to be in memory. But with *Home of the Brave* you'd talked yourself into a whole feature show.

ANDERSON: Well, one reason was that for the first time I had a manager and he said, "Wouldn't you rather be recording and other things instead of touring so much? Why don't you do a short tour, and make a film of it?" And I thought that would be exciting. It was also a really hard time, because on the *Mr. Heartbreak* tour we had gotten completely out of hand and lost a huge amount of

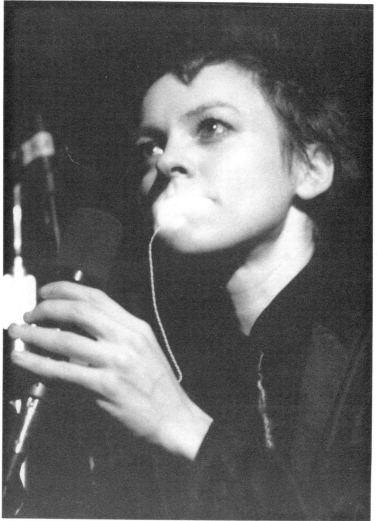

With a small light in her mouth, Anderson emits an otherworldly glow.

money. I was totally in debt from the tour because it involved thir-ty-five people.

HOWELL: *Mr. Heartbreak* was the tour that was the bulk of *Home of the Brave.*

ANDERSON: Right. It went to Japan and around the United States, but not to Europe because at that point we were so broke. It wasn't the manager's fault; it was my fault for making the deal the way I did, which was that he would get paid no matter what and I would absorb the production cost. So he ended up making a huge amount of money and I went way into debt. It should have made money because we went to a lot of different places. We worked really hard. We did shows almost every night.

HOWELL: It's so hard to make money touring.

ANDERSON: Oh, *man!*

HOWELL: You discovered the economics of touring.

ANDERSON: I discovered the mismanagement of touring economics. You don't have to go in the hole.

HOWELL: *United States* was a more subsidized kind of thing. BAM [Brooklyn Academy of Music] wanted it. People wanted it, so they put up money. So there were anchor points.

ANDERSON: There were, yes. It wasn't as totally risky as depending on box office.

HOWELL: Which is what happened after *United States,* when it is more pop world, how many tickets you can sell is what you make.

ANDERSON: And I was also really clear that I didn't want to do grants. Grants are for people starting out, and I had gotten a lot of help from grants—NEA and a bunch of New York state council things. If I can do box office, I've got no business taking grants. And I felt a little bit that way about commissions, too, though not quite as much. Because I admired places like DC Space. I loved the way they set up their gallery. They had a restaurant, and the restaurant would support the gallery; they wouldn't have to worry about getting grants from anybody. They could do whatever they wanted. That worked really well for years, because they loved cooking and eating and they were really good at it. And I thought, "This is so hip." Have an arm of your work that's strictly commercial and supports the other thing.

HOWELL: Artspace in San Francisco is like that. They have a restaurant.

ANDERSON: Uh-huh, it's a great idea. People love to eat and why be squabbling over this rather small amount of money when you can get a business happening? So that was sort of my model—DC Space. I quickly discovered that I had no commercial skills whatsoever. (Laughs.)

HOWELL: So then there was another album and another tour, but everything was done quite differently.

ANDERSON: Well, also at the time the film came out, the other part of the strategy was to do the film's opening and a tour together. And I also got talked into this by this manager; up to that point, I'd always thought, "What would I really enjoy doing?" and this was more like, "Here's how we can *strategize*." And so he said, "Do a tour of songs that you've already done; plenty of people do a greatest hits tour, just do that." I was really exhausted from cutting the movie, and he thought, "Tour this new show when the movie comes out."

HOWELL: Support the movie.

ANDERSON: Yeah. And I said, "Well, let me try to put that together." That became the *Natural History* tour. It was really hard to do; I wasn't ready to do a tour again.

HOWELL: I remember the show at the Beacon in 1986. It was big and complicated.

ANDERSON: That was *Mr. Heartbreak*. It wasn't the *Natural History* tour.

HOWELL: *Natural History* had a lot of bouncy music to it and some tropical things—everything that your mood *wasn't*. (Laughs.)

ANDERSON: It had a best-forgotten song called "Whose Shoes" in it— plenty of these songs did not get recorded. I was going on this tour and it was supposed to be the greatest hits tour but I thought, "Well, I've got to write a few new things." So I wrote "Baby Doll" and "Whose Shoes." Ay, ay, ay! I was trying to sing, and I didn't know how to sing it right at all. It was just humiliating.

HOWELL: What makes you want to bury a song like that? Do you just look at it and automatically recoil from everything about it?

ANDERSON: Yeah, pretty much. And I was so self-conscious. I wanted to do a thing about salesmanship, but it was written in rehearsals and the guys would sing some things and say a lot of stuff during the song, so it jumped away from my control. There were a couple of parts that were in my own voice but mostly they were in this screechy, overpushed voice.

HOWELL: I asked Phil [Glass] once, "Do you ever write turkeys?" He said, "Oh, yeah." Then I said, "Do you ever perform them?" And he said, "Rarely." So I asked him why, and he said, "Well, I know I've written a bad piece when the band stops playing and starts laughing. It kind of helps me." But I think that it is doing something in a negative way that defines what you do well.

ANDERSON: Yes, it is. I remember having a long conversation with Roma after that tour; she just said, "Don't do that again." She had just given me really good advice on a solo tour. She said, "If you want to do old stuff, do real simple versions." I didn't have the nerve to do it; it was a bad call on my part.

HOWELL: Was part of that because you had become part of the pop world, so people expected spectacles?

ANDERSON: Yes, they did. But I realize that the most important things in these shows are just a few images you get, and mostly they can be spoken. Mostly, they can be expressed with just a voice—really nothing else. So that's what I'm trying to think of: How can I do that? Is that going to be possible? And then I had this frightening moment in Madrid in December [1991]. I was supposed to go to a press conference for a show in Seville [*at the World Exposition in 1992—JH*], and I didn't have a title—I didn't even know what it was going to be about. I had just done an interview with John Cage for *Tricycle*, and I had mentioned I was going to Madrid and that I didn't have any idea what I was doing, and he just started laughing. And I thought, "Isn't this delightful? It *is* funny that I don't know any of this." It cheered me up. Then I got there and there were thirty TV stations and it wasn't funny at all. (Laughs.) Not the least bit funny. So I tried to think, "How would John Cage deal with this? He would just laugh." I tried to make myself laugh, but I couldn't. It was just a nightmare.

HOWELL: Well, you know, people take art very seriously. They have expectations of artists that they don't expect from people in real life. An artist is supposed to be articulate. You're supposed to have a name, a production date, all of that. And it never occurs to them that none of those things might be there. That makes them very alarmed.

ANDERSON: It leaves them with absolutely nothing to do. Absolutely nothing. They can't even typeset their program. (Laughs.)

HOWELL: You could have said, "The name is *Canal Street 1992*. It's about the changes in life in America today," or, "It's about a new kitten I got and what I learned about animals." Anything, *please.* (Laughs.)

ANDERSON: But saying nothing at all was really too shocking for them.

HOWELL: People who don't think about how artists really live and work, don't think about those problems. It's kind of a what-have-you-done-for-me-lately thing. You know, everything should be getting better all the time. For example, *Stop Making Sense* not only summed up everything Talking Heads did, it so reinterpreted and sealed it that they couldn't think of what else to do after. They just put it in neutral and made a couple of vernacular records while they tried to figure a way out of it—and they couldn't. Things have a natural life, and they have a momentum.

ANDERSON: They do. They really do. And you have to figure out a way to go on. It's interesting watching what David [Byrne] is doing now. I admire all the different kinds of stuff he's up to. I really liked the orchestral version of *The Forest [an opera Byrne composed in collaboration with director Robert Wilson—JH]* . He seems to come up with things that keep moving along in some way. I mean, you die if you live in the past.

HOWELL: Wasn't it Faulkner who said, "The past isn't dead yet; the past isn't even over?" I think he was making a case for this blob of Bergsonian consciousness where the past is rammed in your brain along with everything else and comes up in flickers and shards and fragments. It interacts with what we think is the present.

ANDERSON: Well, it'll do that anyway, but if you actually try to go back—

HOWELL: What does going back mean for you?

ANDERSON: Right now, going back means doing this archive book [*a catalog documenting her career—JH*]. If I could do it in an impersonal way as an editor, it would really be fine, but I look at these photographs and see in the background my friends from that time helping me do something, and I go, "Oh my God, where is he now?" It's very distracting. And all these people I used to know in Europe, I've always thought that someday I'm going to take a year and go to all the cities that I've been in and find those people again. I don't think I could.

HOWELL: Because they would talk about their contact with you, which was that performance they saw.

Bill Graham and Avalon Present

An Evening With

Laurie
Anderson

Perkins Palace, Pasadena
Friday & Saturday
March 18 & 19, 8 PM
Tickets: $11 reserved, all seats

Tickets available at all usual outlets.

The hi-tech aura of the performance is balanced by Anderson's relaxed,
intimate stage persona.

ANDERSON: I got a note from someone when I was in Miami [*doing* Voices From the Beyond *in 1991—JH*]; it was a letter that he had written during my talk, which was three hours long. This letter was from someone who said, "I know you remember me; it was in San Francisco in 1980-something. We stayed up all night and talked about music and films. Remember the smell of the jasmine?" And I was like, "No, I don't. Who is this?" (Laughs.) I didn't see his face ever, and it was this long letter—it was almost unbearable to get it.

HOWELL: But this is something we wanted from what we call performance art. We didn't want impersonal art. We didn't want something you could be objective about. We wanted the contact. Boy, do we have it. (Laughs.) And, as with any performer, there are lots of people who have no idea who you are, but they think they do. They hear your record, they see you talk and perform— and they identify with you. "I know her. She's saying what I thought, so she knows *me*."

ANDERSON: Well, apparently, it had been more than that in this case. (Laughs.)

HOWELL: The jasmine...we could conjure up quite a scene here. (Laughs.)

ANDERSON: I was trying to fill in the blanks, but I couldn't.

HOWELL: We were talking about memory flickers. It seems like a lot of your songs involve those. You start *Voices from the Beyond* talking about your grandmother. You revisit the past in some ways.

ANDERSON: Yes, occasionally I try to slip it in, in this case to try to understand what the future means. There's projection involved in the past, too.

HOWELL: There was an article in the *New York Times* about memory. It's loose, all over your brain. If you can't recall that night in San Francisco, it's simply misfiled. It's in the computer under the wrong heading.

ANDERSON: Yeah, mine wasn't under jasmine. (Laughs.)

HOWELL: We talked earlier about your first shows and the kind of charm of the crudeness of the technology. It's clear that the technology mattered, but your manipulation of it was a transparent union with practicality. You had no money, so you had the super-8 thing; you had no help, so you punched the button yourself. It became part of the show. And then things got more ambitious.

ANDERSON: They got more complicated.

HOWELL: And you became Miss Technology.

ANDERSON: That was my rep for a while.

HOWELL: Was that something you set out to do, or were you surprised to discover that you had become so involved with technology. Did you see gadgets and want them?

ANDERSON: Yes, I did. I saw gadgets and I wanted them. It was really simple. I just love tricks. And then I would find a way to use them. I love electronics. It's eerie.

HOWELL: You mention in this book documenting *Empty Places* that storytellers gather around the fire and, for you, electronics has the mystery and power of fire.

ANDERSON: Yes, that's true. Although in my next thing, there are going to be little fires on the stage. Just little fires burning. Nothing's plugged in.

HOWELL: I remember certain of your shows where the feeling was, "What kind of gadget is going to come out of her pocket?" There was a guy on "Captain Kangaroo" called the Bananaman; he had a suit with huge pockets and he would pull bananas out and little folding cardboard boxes to hold the bananas, until eventually he had an entire train full of bananas, and it would just drive off. When you adopted the suit, I thought it was like the Bananaman. Here comes the weird violin. Here comes the percussion-suit. They were sort of wondrous, sometimes obvious.

ANDERSON: It's the disappearing body. That's why I had it in the show.

HOWELL: You were the prop to activate these objects.

ANDERSON: Yes, I wanted to disappear in the same way, to use similar mechanics.

HOWELL: Why did you want to disappear?

ANDERSON: I thought disembodied stories were more interesting, for the same reason that I hate theater. I hate all those bodies onstage. It's too real.

HOWELL: Did you feel that direct storytelling became too quickly or too easily intimate?

ANDERSON: Well, no. I liked part of that but I didn't want to be so physical about it. Later there were sort of dancing-around things, but that was another issue. Mostly that was the reason to dress[in white], to project on that and become invisible. And that was also the reason I wore all black for a while. Well, that probably wasn't the only reason—everybody wore all black then—but I wanted to blend into the shadows. I was scared that it would be some kind of stand-up shtick, and I wanted the main thing to be the words—then I would be off to the side.

HOWELL: A lot of the gadgets had to do with altering your voice, which was another way to disembody it from you.

ANDERSON: That was just, you know, a puppet show. And also just an exercise to try to find another point of view. If I spoke in a totally different way, I would find that I thought in a totally different way.

HOWELL: For a long time your shows were solo. Being solo is a way to have more presence.

ANDERSON: But you get incredibly bored with your own voice and your own point of view too. So that [the gadgets and altering the voice] was a way to shake myself out of that.

HOWELL: Some of these gadgets...well, "inventions" sounds a little more important—

ANDERSON: —No, "gadgets" sounds good! (Laughs)

HOWELL: Some of them have an independent life. Are they still loose out in the world, apart from you?

ANDERSON: I was in Athens about a year ago and some Greek collector said, "Come over to my house for dinner and look at my collection." Jeffrey Deitch [*art consultant—JH*] had done all these catalogs of this man's exhibitions. I looked around, and over in the corner was this phone booth I'd made. I had no idea what had ever happened to this thing, and there it was, sitting over there in Athens. And it was still working. The tape was still going around—he had it plugged in and every-

At some point I was using gadgets as defense. I had to have a huge distance—it was too scary.

thing. It looked pretty good. I have a couple of those around still. There's a self-turning book in my basement. It had been in storage in all sorts of different places. Pretty chaotic.

HOWELL: The technology got to a point where some of the audience wanted more contact with you. Some people got a little impatient with all of—

ANDERSON: —with all of the tricks, yes. Well, at some point I was using the gadgets as a defense.

HOWELL: You were keeping the audience back?

ANDERSON: Yes. There was a time when I thought, "I'm going to get eaten alive." That was in the mid-eighties. I thought I had to have a huge distance, because it was too scary.

HOWELL: Up until then, there was a balance between storytelling and device.

ANDERSON: Yes. Then I went into technicolor.

HOWELL: Techno-obsession. Did you feel exposed, like you didn't want the kind of contact that you'd had before?

ANDERSON: It wasn't the contact. It was the expectations. It was really exhausting being rushed around in limos and doing press interviews all over Europe, day after day, either as part of a tour or just for press. I'd sit in a room—they should have had a lie detector thing there. (Laughs.) Because it would start at eight in the morning and go till eleven at night, and every half-hour or forty-five minutes someone else would come in and ask the exact same question. It was an exquisite form of torture, because I would try to invent new answers or say things slightly differently, but they would all ask the same questions. It would always start out with: "How do you feel about being in the pop world?" And as the day wore on, I felt worse and worse about being in the pop world. (Laughs.) It was so debilitating to talk about myself all day—for days.

HOWELL: You've talked about the subliminal adjustment you felt you were making for the pop world—they wanted a spectacle, they had expectations of something bigger than you'd already done. After *Natural History*, you went back to a more solo performance with *Empty Places*. It was just you onstage, but there were seventeen people on the crew and two trucks.

ANDERSON: Yeah, that's the solo show. (Laughs.)

HOWELL: When you went back to being solo, you had obviously metamorphosed through these larger shows, which were technically more officious and more complicated. Yet I remember when I saw *Empty Places* at BAM, there was some kind of disorientation you were attributing to the fact that you were one person in the middle of this giant electronic force field.

ANDERSON: Disorientation. Well, I was also very sick.

HOWELL: Did you make a speech from the stage, something about the force field? Didn't you say something about going to see an acupuncturist?

ANDERSON: I did go to see an acupuncturist, but the speech wasn't in that show. It was in *Voices from the Beyond*.

HOWELL: That's right, it was a catch-up story.

ANDERSON: He [the acupuncturist] drew a force field on the keyboard stand. Actually, what happened was that all the cables were inside of the keyboard stand—which would roll on a platform so you could get up on it—and it wasn't grounded, so I was constantly getting low-level shocks. The keyboard stand would roll and lock into position, but it felt like it was going to skid into the audience. So it was a combination of feeling very dizzy, getting low-level shocks, and feeling like I was going to roll into the first row. And I was already ill. I felt very, very disoriented.

HOWELL: So it wasn't grounded, and that ungrounded you.

ANDERSON: Yeah. So this acupuncturist—I'll never live this down with the stage hands—made up a five-pointed star that he wanted engraved in metal on the keyboard stand as a grounding device.

HOWELL: And what happened?

ANDERSON: Because he said it would work, I felt a little better—but I'm sure it didn't do a single thing. We also happened to ground the thing.

HOWELL: Practically, in Western materialist terms. The wires were literally grounded. But then you had the cosmic acupuncturist, so you had both ends covered.

ANDERSON: Yeah. (Laughs.) I never really quite understood that disease I had; it was a very weird one, kind of like food poisoning or something, that went on for about a year. I thought I was losing my mind, but since other people who were on tour with me got it, too, it was a little less terrifying. I would just get up and feel like I was going to fall down. Things were out of focus. I'd walk down the street and everything would look unreal. It's like this great description of [the drug] Halcion that I read in the *Times*. "As if an angel of the Lord comes into your bedroom and tells you that nothing matters and that everything you're worried about is happening on Mars." And it's perfect.

HOWELL: You have to be careful saying that around sixties kids; it doesn't sound like a bad idea sometimes. (Laughs.)

ANDERSON: When you're negotiating cars in Japan, Mars just doesn't blend in with the idea. (Laughs.) You need to be thinking "down at the mall"—grounded.

HOWELL: You also said what you intended to do was drag a lot of equipment that normally stays in studios, or behind the scenes, onto the stage. Then see how it worked, to see what else you could do with it. To experiment. I've seen at least two or three times when there've been major technological problems. One time, you came up on a platform and I guess it pulled a wire loose, so your background vocals didn't come on. Sometimes the audience doesn't know something's wrong unless you communicate that to them. Other times something's wrong, but for you that's part of the moment. This is performance art that has incorporated the John Cage idea. But at the same time, you plan and rehearse, and you want it to be a certain way. Then the chorus drops out because the machine won't come on. I guess you got about four or five minutes into it, then they popped it on. Nobody thought two seconds about it. I don't know if you did or not.

ANDERSON: I didn't really. It didn't bother me. It was very freeing in a way, to just go, "Why don't I pretend I'm playing keyboards and not bring all this stuff? Have people *think* the melody."

HOWELL: Are you really as insouciant as you say in your book, where those problems are just part of what happens in performance? Or is that something you've had to will yourself to accept?

ANDERSON: There's no way you can completely guard yourself against it, so you have to be prepared, and you might as well have a good time instead of feeling humiliated or apologetic.

HOWELL: Well, audiences will feel how you do.

ANDERSON: Yeah, they will.

HOWELL: If you feel embarrassed and distraught they will, too.

ANDERSON: Or you can say, "Hey, this is fun! Now *you* sing the keyboard part, here's how it goes. Let's see how many tenors we have here."

HOWELL: In *Voices from the Beyond*, the tech level has dropped dramatically.

ANDERSON: To just about zilch.

HOWELL: There's a slide, there's a microphone, there's three songs, and talking, and a notebook.

ANDERSON: And that's it.

HOWELL: So now your tech is drained out. There has to be some marriage of practicality. You can put it all in a suitcase and go do it.

ANDERSON: That's been the reason for simplifying this performance

[*Voices from the Beyond*]. It's infinitely expandable and it can talk about whatever just happened. And since it's heavily about politics, I find it much more interesting than what's happening in the art world. I don't know if it's a work of art, but I don't care. It seems like everybody thinks they're alone in their opinions, and they're really shocked when somebody stands up and goes, "Blah, blah, blah, blah! Blah, blah, blah!" I especially got that in Miami. People were astounded that they could relate to what I was saying and that it wasn't deeply different from anything they had heard in the last year about current events. And all of these other people around them had also thought that they were the only ones who felt that way...Image-making in this country is just so powerful; when you have an incredibly biased media and it's basically sending out well-designed—I guess you'd have to call them propagandist—images, there's no way to challenge those except through words. And it's quite easy to do, because when you just look at what they are actually saying, it's very easy to pick apart.

HOWELL: In this show you offer people just one kind of image, whereas in the past they've come to expect multiple images and correlation. Now there is one slide, a lot of talking, then you go over and sing, then there's more talking.

ANDERSON: It's all words really. The music is very incidental. Even though I've been doing a lot of recording lately, I'm not quite sure what I'm going to use it for. I've been doing a lot of getting stuff together—trying to trick myself into an album, I think.

HOWELL: Is it possible that by stripping some of the music out of the show, it's flowing over into the recording? Is it easier to record when you're not performing it?

ANDERSON: Yes, although performing is the easiest way to make it simple; I could sit in a studio and make something really complicated that could take years to do. *Strange Angels* took two years. Before that, I'd worked out songs in shows and, if they were interesting enough, I'd add a few more things and that would become the album. *Strange Angels* was a studio-produced album from the beginning. There was only one song that had ever been performed.

HOWELL: You said that *Voices from the Beyond* is a kind of add-and-subtract show, a run-on show, and you're not even sure if it's art.

ANDERSON: That is definitely what I like about it.

HOWELL: So if you want to say something about Iraq, you just go

Sound poet John Giorno toured with Anderson and William Burroughs.

straight to the talking part; there's no song leading up to it. Do you feel that's more appropriate to the seriousness of the material, or is that just how you want to present it right now?

ANDERSON: It's a little of both. I can't work fast enough to get all of these ideas into images and songs, because I can't possibly keep up with the bizarre twists of what's happening on a daily basis. So I want to do something that's not quite so tied to the headlines, but I have to figure out some other form, without going back to what I was doing before. One of the things I just did was re-read Thomas Pynchon's book, *Gravity's Rainbow*. He's such a great author. I'd love to work with that book.

HOWELL: Have you ever based a show on someone else's material?

ANDERSON: No. And I think it could be a really interesting way to do things. I may go back and read the book with that in mind, and think, "No, I've got my own paranoia. I don't need to touch this guy's." (Laughs.)

HOWELL: Is *Voices from the Beyond* a sort of transitional movement until you figure out the next way you want to appear?

ANDERSON: Maybe not. I try not to assign a value to this. I've watched other artists, like Wim Wenders, who works on big projects for years, then he can't get the money or something, so he just does something else in the meantime—some kind of throw-away thing—and it's much better, because it is fresh.

HOWELL: He takes the pressure off of himself.

ANDERSON: Yes. It doesn't have to be his masterwork. So I try to have that attitude. I try to be free enough to try something, not to clutch like I really have to achieve something.

HOWELL: People constantly comment on your haircut. I can't find an article that doesn't mention the spiky punk haircut. Is that unusual among women? Do you think people were reading some kind of wild symbolism into it?

ANDERSON: At first the comment was, "It looks like she's just been electrocuted," or something like that. It was part of electronics somehow, the haircut you got from sticking your finger in a socket. (Laughs.) Somebody mentioned it at a book-signing; they said, "You look exactly like I thought you would." And I thought, "Oh, God. I should at least wear a hat or something."

HOWELL: I think it has something to do with the way people started reading you in pop terms. They read performers clothes and hair.

It means something. They read hair as a code, so when you went from the white dress to the suit then back to white again, people were reading all sorts of moods and intentions.

ANDERSON: And they were right, too. That's the thing. They were actually more right than I was.

HOWELL: You weren't aware they were reading it that way?

ANDERSON: I kind of was. Like I said before, it was about hid-

There is one personal thing in Home of the Brave. Otherwise, it's about: "Don't get near me."

ing. When I wore that white minstrel outfit from this kind of Vegas era, I was hiding behind that showman thing.

HOWELL: Hiding behind being very visible.

ANDERSON: Right, yeah. And there's one personal thing in *Home of the Brave*—the white lilies. Otherwise it's about: "Don't you dare get near me. I'm like an automaton." I really tried to do that with the masks and the mechanical stuff. And a lot of the images were communication by remote, radar—things that were very removed or campy in a way, like the silver lame dress that I wore.

HOWELL: With sneakers.

ANDERSON: Well, I had to wear sneakers. No way I wanted to be Vegas completely.

HOWELL: Do you feel now, when you do *Voices from the Beyond*, that you appear to be a little closer to "yourself"?

ANDERSON: I wear what I would wear of an evening. Maybe a little bit more dressed up, but nothing special. Not a costume. It's really a lot like the performances in 1976. I really made a point of not looking special in any way. Just street clothes and words. That was supposed to be it. I think I thought I was a poet or something.

HOWELL: There was also a strong ethic in the art world at that time.

ANDERSON: Yes, there was.

HOWELL: Performance art was supposed to destroy theatricality and distance and illusion. I'm "me" or a version of me, but I'm *more* me.

ANDERSON: All the Trisha Brown dancers wore those baggy pants anyway. And I loved that. It was the workers' uniform of SoHo. Kind of dance-like outfits or sweats or jeans. You never had to change your clothes.

HOWELL: When I first saw you, you were in the sixties mock-military mode—jeans and a fatigue jacket. It was a thing we used to do because it was cheap. It was a uniform.

ANDERSON: Yeah, it was left over from my days as a sculptor, really. Work clothes. I was doing a lot of hammering and stuff like that. I was making these talking boxes up on stilts and working with wood and polyurethane. That's how you dress for that.

HOWELL: But the haircut persists.

ANDERSON: I tried to do something else, because I feel so different. Maybe I'll get a moustache going. That would be fun to do. (Laughs.)

HOWELL: When you perform, do you consciously feel like "you" but in an amplified kind of way? Or is there some feeling that you're something else entirely when you go out there?

ANDERSON: It depends on what I'm doing. With *Voices from the Beyond*, I could go offstage and talk to people normally and I didn't have to switch gears at all. It was very similar to the way I talk anyway.

HOWELL: Was that because of the subject matter?

ANDERSON: Yeah. It was totally contemporary stuff—What happened in the news today?—and it wasn't going through any filters. Now I'm writing a piece, *Halcion Days: Stories from the Nerve Bible*. I hate titles worse than anything, but they always put a gun to my head and say, "We're cancelling your contract unless you give us a title in the next five minutes." So for this piece, I got out Pictionary, shuffled all the cards around, and put them all over the floor. I came up with a bunch of titles. None of them really worked, though. There was *Wagon Train Repair Man;* it didn't seem to work very well, although it would have been: "Yes, I'm a wagon train repair man. Damn those Japanese. I just cannot get work. I work as a wagon train repair man. I just haven't been able to get anything steady lately." And *Diet Confetti* didn't seem to apply. *Kosher Phone Booths* was sort of nice, but it didn't really apply, either. *Skid Row Stepdaughter* was kind of nice—maybe I'll make that a film sometime.

HOWELL: Will this new piece work like *Voices from the Beyond*, where you were talking more like yourself?

ANDERSON: I wish I knew. It's a big struggle right now, because I'm adding up all these images. I just collect stuff. I have a vague idea what it's going to be about so I think, "Well, I really want to start with Desert Storm." What does that mean? What is this kind of fury that happens over there, near the little old town of Bethlehem, rock-throwing capital of the world? Why are we there? Is there some kind of desert urge in this country? I think there might be. A burning bush kind of deal. So I thought, "Hmmm, a tornado would be a nice image." So that's why we built this twelve-foot-high working tornado, bringing our own weather there. A lot of the stuff starts with technical things. You know, I thought, "Well, I hate rectangles; I'm really tired of projecting onto rectangles," so I started working with a globe. Projecting onto a globe, projecting onto cylinders. That actually started because I was trying to make fake holograms.

HOWELL: Cheap holograms.

ANDERSON: Cheap *and* fake. Well, I was actually going to make some real ones, so I went to see a friend of mine who makes holograms, and they don't work on the stage. Not at all. And that's the most fun of holograms—watching people watch them, and the little dance they do. Up, down, left, right—trying to see how it changes. So I decided to go back to the low-tech way of doing it. That became this other projection system, and the imagery kind of came from that. Crystal balls and dead sea squirrels and things that wrap around things.

HOWELL: These are all very personal things. On any given day, reading the newspaper or looking at TV, there are any number of things you could pick out. You may be just collecting things, but you're collecting very *specific* things, no?

ANDERSON: Well, most of them are. But when I shoot something like that artist-bunny [*a huge blown-up photographic image of a rabbit wearing a beret and carrying a palette, inside of a small plastic snow globe, to be used in* Halcion Days—*JH*], I do it just because it's really pretty and I love stuff that sloshes around like that. Otherwise you're just writing a script and then illustrating it. That never worked for me. I always thought, "Vaguely, I want to talk about language. Vaguely, I want to talk about authority." Various themes interest me, so I kind of make a pool of images and see what happens. Right now they're sort of splattered all over the floor—I have these odd pieces of tape and images that could go any which way. I had seen a set design that looked like a falling meteorite had just missed a house, and I thought, "Oh, this is great—I'll have a giant meteor come down in my next show." But it looked kind of silly when it just missed a toy house on a stage, so I had it come down on a keyboard and play a massive chord.

HOWELL: In a lot of your work there are things that are scavenged from TV or news—or you often say, "Somebody told me about..." or "I heard about..."—but there are other things that seem to come more out of the subconscious or out of dreams or funny visions. Does much of your material come from that?

ANDERSON: Yeah, and it's a three A.M. situation. That's how I write at three A.M.

HOWELL: Half-awake, half-asleep.

ANDERSON: No defenses. I record the stuff and listen to it the next day and go, "Wait a second. What's that supposed to be about?" Maybe one thing out of fifty will be sort of interesting, and I'll pick that when I'm back in a rational mood.

HOWELL: What makes it interesting?

ANDERSON: That it's really tilted in a direction that's so odd. That it almost comes out of babbling, let's say. That you babble for an hour, play the keyboards, bring a bunch of different sounds in, turn on some projectors and babble.

HOWELL: And in that babble you find some nugget that won't let go of you.

ANDERSON: It won't go away, yeah. And then that gets circled somehow.

HOWELL: Is it hard to have access? I mean, do you have to stay up till three, drink a lot of coffee, and get into a certain state to allow that thing to develop—otherwise it's inaccessible?

ANDERSON: Yeah. It's totally inaccessible. I can't sit down at a word processor and do that at all.

HOWELL: I think it was Fitzgerald who wrote something about the three A.M. of the soul. If you didn't go to sleep by three, you missed the point when you should have gone to sleep—and now you're awake in a different state.

ANDERSON: It's really true. That's why a lot of my early stuff used to be called things like *Songs and Stories for the Insomniac*, because I would always do that. Now I don't stay up all night as much, but I can actually get into that state sometimes in the afternoon now. If I shut the door and all the windows and pretend it's night, I can trick myself.

HOWELL: Do you actually record dreams? Do you write them down?

ANDERSON: My actual dreams are not very interesting, the ones that I have when I'm asleep. I dream I'm grocery shopping but I'm flying. Just what everyone dreams about.

HOWELL: So it's this half-awake, half-asleep thing that's a little more interesting.

ANDERSON: Yeah. Half of my dreams are pretty paranoid and half of them are pretty joyful—except for the flying/shopping dreams, which are just the convenience things. I think that would be really nice, to just fly with a couple of bags, fly out of my window and—

HOWELL: —get the food here faster.

ANDERSON: Yeah. Those are kind of improvement dreams. How to improve things.

HOWELL: Another assumption about performance artists is that a lot of what they do is self-expression. They have dreams, they have experiences, they have opinions. And the work consists of that more than it does in regular theatre or music.

ANDERSON: Self-expression is a big word, though, and I bet a lot of people would think of performance art in a broader way. If I were really just expressing myself, I wouldn't think that people would be that interested. I try to pick things that would make people say, "I was just thinking that a couple of days ago; I didn't say it exactly like that but I had that idea." They do think these things; they just don't choose to pursue it in the same way.

I don't believe the function of art is to make this a more fair place. I think it is to make it a more delightful place—but that's different.

HOWELL: It's not their job.

ANDERSON: It's not their job, or it's something that's noticed and doesn't have to be articulated, but it is felt.

HOWELL: What happens when you articulate that?

ANDERSON: They think I'm mind-reading. They really do.

HOWELL: Those subjects are in the air and you're bringing them together in a certain way for people. This is always a thing that gets thrown up when people directly address politics: Should art be about politics? If so, is it supposed to change things or just be a flag for it? Is that asking too much of art?

ANDERSON: I don't believe that's really the function of art, to make this a more fair place. I think it's to make it a more delightful place, but that's totally different. I've noticed in the group that I've been working with—the Women's Action Coalition—that there is something really disheartening about always having to be PC [politically correct], because things aren't really like that. On the level of law they are, but below that, there are much more interesting areas that are not as clear as how we try to define them in a political context. It feels a little crude to be working that way. One of our biggest goals—along with a lot of other women's groups—is to try to resurrect the Equal Rights Amendment. I pretty much figure that anything else you do doesn't really matter unless that law is in place—equal rights for women. And there is no such thing now. It's just unbelievable to me that it doesn't exist, but it does not. The last time it came up was 1983 and Reagan said, "You don't need it. You've already got all this stuff." In the last ten years, I've felt it in very direct ways. This backlash deal is very real. Yet, at the same time, things are more complicated than that on another level. So, as an artist, I really have to be careful about getting too strident.

HOWELL: Would you say it's been more difficult for you because you are a woman artist?

ANDERSON: It's harder for women doctors, for women lawyers, for women *period*. Of course it's more difficult for women artists. Not very many women are complaining about this, and I wish they were.

HOWELL: Why aren't they complaining?

ANDERSON: For the same reasons that they have low self-esteem, and everything that comes from that.

HOWELL: So you think there was a big fight in the seventies—women made a lot of agitation and things seemed to change—but in the nineties it is worse?

ANDERSON: It really is worse than it was in the seventies.

HOWELL: Because people are quiet. They go about their business, because they think they didn't get anything for yelling.

ANDERSON: Yeah. And I think in many ways women are genuinely more conservative—that's part of it, too. Let's just try to work this out as it is. Let's not rip everything apart. I mean, I didn't understand the phrase "deep denial" until I watched some women's reactions to Anita Hill and to William Kennedy Smith or the Tyson thing, [these women] forgetting what it's like to be a teenager [as was Tyson's victim] when you don't really know what you want or you get excited about things and think, "Oh boy, I'm going to

At times Anderson seems diminutive as compared to the power of her sound and visuals.

bring my Brownie camera and see movie stars." You forget that you were that stupid, that…you were that naive and that fresh.

HOWELL: The criticism of Desirée Washington seemed to be: "How could you be that stupid?" But she's eighteen years old.

ANDERSON: She's a teenager.

HOWELL: Well, remember those seventies questions that came up? Did women artists have to be women first and then artists? Or could they be artists who then had a sex? Could they be a person first? Remember those chicken-and-egg kind of discussions?

ANDERSON: I do. I definitely do. My whole definition of myself has changed in the last couple of years. I used to say, when anyone would ask, "First I'm an artist, then I'm a New Yorker, and third I'm a woman." Now I would say, "First I'm an artist, then I'm a woman, and third I'm a New Yorker." It hasn't changed that much, but it's a lot for me. This last year [1991] really shook me up, watching how women are treated. It really did. I was just so furious. I haven't been that angry at things for a long time. With the sex battles and trials I thought, "How could this cruelty be happening?"

HOWELL: Has there been—or will there be—something that could be identified as a specific female point of view in your performances? I mean, has being a woman been a major factor in your work?

ANDERSON: That's a good question. I always try basically to do both, to be a narrator and then to go to the woman's point of view and the man's point of view. I always thought that was fair. I have never been someone who would just prance on in a big, fluffy skirt and be a female.

HOWELL: You did once in *Home of the Brave*.

ANDERSON: That was an exception, and I felt more in drag than I had ever felt wearing pants in SoHo. Just look at any female artist. We don't wear dresses. Here are some [*Harpers* Index] statistics: Chances that an American woman considers herself a strong supporter of the women's movement—one in five; average percentage change in an American man's standard of living in the year after a divorce—plus forty-three; average change in a woman's standard of living—minus seventy-three. Percentage of American women who said in 1970 that men were basically "kind, gentle and thoughtful"—sixty-seven; percentage who say this in 1992—

fifty-one. It's dropping. Jenny Holzer [a visual artist] says, "Men don't protect anymore." They never did. Not really.

HOWELL: It was in the culture, some idea that they should. It would be embarrassing if they didn't. Other men would think less of them.

ANDERSON: Protecting exactly what and who? And what was the fall-out? As soon as women began to challenge some of the authority of men, [seeking their protection] was just unthinkable.

HOWELL: That shows you how much of the protection was about protecting privilege.

ANDERSON: Exactly. That's what it seems to be about. And for women this is a big shock. I think that's why the Anita Hill thing was just so revealing for a lot of women. Here's a woman who dared to say, "I want power, too," basically. "I want to keep my job and rise in it. I want to do *your* job." That was so unthinkable to the Senate committee that they hit on, "Oh! She was in love with him. That would explain it. She's in love with a guy like us, a man in power like we are. Of course, we're lovable and desirable." In fact, it had nothing to do with that. I mean there are many possible scenarios and I know there are lots of dark tales under it, and trades that went on, but I see it basically that way.

HOWELL: It sounds like your whole stance is being altered. In the seventies, when you started performing, there was a lot of ferment about it. Did you feel an awareness then?

ANDERSON: I was part of a women's group in the seventies, but it was very unsatisfying for me. That's when I started doing political pamphlets.

HOWELL: Why was it unsatisfying?

ANDERSON: Because we'd have a lot of meetings and it was all women artists saying, "The gallery system is corrupt; the collecting system is corrupt." Without even waiting a beat. It was "Men have everything, how do we get it? How do we get as corrupt as the men?" And I thought, "Wait a minute, girls. Do you want to design something new or do you want to just move in? And if you think it's so bad let's think of some other way to do it." There was a very feeble effort at cooperative female galleries that, of course, nobody cared about. Nobody ever came to the shows. It was occasionally suggested, in the seventies, that I was definitively female because I used circular images like the oversized round lens I designed. I've never heard of a square lens. I decided, "I'm not going to have any more to do with this categorization of things as male or female. I'm going to work it out in my own way and try to look at the world from as many different points of view as I can. Change my voice in as many different ways as I can and not identify so strongly with who I am. Narrate. Narrate." And so, when I narrated things as myself in the early seventies, it was always shy-Midwestern-girl-tells-all. It was like that was the persona, but that was never really what I thought I was doing.

HOWELL: Was there not another seduction level because a woman was doing it? Men appreciate shy confessions.

ANDERSON: Right, yeah. And so do women. That was one of the aspects of who I was. But I sometimes used it as a kind of puppet

As a child, I was always aware that there was an imposter in my family's house who looked exactly like me and would do civilized things, but I myself was free to see the real stuff.

as well, because I was trying to speak from another place. As a child I was, too. When I would ride my bike up and down the streets in Glen Ellyn [Illinois], I'd stop once in a while and pick a scab or pick my nose, then I'd get back on my bike and ride around, I was always very aware that there was an imposter who lived in my family's house and looked exactly like me and would do civilized things like go to school and learn things and be a good family member and so on, but that I *myself* was free to ride around and see the real stuff. That bike was really important to me. And I still feel like that. I learn a lot of things from getting out of my house and traveling. I'm probably just a regular schizophrenic. But I still do feel that I can see the social self I've created and watch it go through its required motions.

HOWELL: But they feel separate to you. As an artist do you think one way and work a different way?

ANDERSON: No, as an artist I also work both ways. I have to be the person on the bike to create it, and then I have to be the person responsible for ordering the equipment and organizing the schedule, all that stuff. But that's true with any artist.

HOWELL: It seems that, unlike some women who appropriate a male persona, your "androgyny" is encompassing. It seems like a translation of voices between the sexes.

ANDERSON: That's what I was trying to do. Because I really have realized that, as a woman, I truly resent not being included in most things that happen officially.

HOWELL: Like what?

ANDERSON: I belong to a nerd computer network called Global Business Network—we're futurists, trying to design things for the future. We actually get paid for this, it's a pretty strange deal. And we get books every month. I got this book, *The Discoverers*, by Daniel Boorstein; I started reading it and, after two or three pages, I burst into tears. I never get this emotional.

HOWELL: What did he say?

ANDERSON: It's about human achievement. It's about all of the bridges and operas and symphonies and formulas and paintings and novels—all done by men. Okay, we have Georgia O'Keeffe and Madame Curie, and we have this tiny handful of others. Women's groups will say we have a lot more than we're ever given credit for, but when I went through the rest of the book just kind of looking to see if any woman was in there, there was only one in the index, out of thousands. I don't even remember who it was. I have always thought of myself as an inventive human being, but I'm not even part of human history. It was devastating to read this thing. I had heard about women having this kind of a reaction to things, but I had always thought, "Oh, come on, don't be so sensitive."

HOWELL: Did you have that reaction when you studied art history ? Did you know there were no women in the Jansen's *History of Art*?

ANDERSON: I knew there were no women, or a couple of token women. I knew it, but I thought that I was special and since I'd never really identified with women in particular—or men, either—I was brought up to think of myself as someone who could achieve something. That was the whole idea. Make something. Do something. And it doesn't matter who you are.

HOWELL: But now you feel like history has been warped because it *does* matter who people are?

ANDERSON: Yes, especially in the past couple of years, with the puritanical twists in this country. I have really been feeling the results of what I truly believe is a disastrous backlash. I've watched women being humiliated, and people feeling that that's okay. I've watched

women hang their heads in courtrooms and say, "Yes sir, no sir, I'm sorry sir." Never stand up and defend themselves, always be meek. And I wanted so much for them to stand up and say, "I have as much right to be here as you do." But it was never that way. Even in the Mike Tyson trial, it wasn't so much that the woman was believed but that white men are afraid of black men. I mean, measuring a black man's dick is an actual, nationally televised sport today.

HOWELL: Did you ever get any special treatment—artistically or personally—for being a woman?

ANDERSON: Probably. I wouldn't be able to say what it is but, for example, when they hand out things like honorary degrees—I've gotten several from various places—I bet they have a kind of thing like, "Shouldn't we give one to a woman?" I'll never know, but I'll bet some heavy money that I got a few prizes because of my sex. That's why I think quotas are a great thing—they're in our favor.

> *I'll bet some heavy money that I got a few prizes because of my sex. That's why I think quotas are a great thing—they're in our favor.*

HOWELL: It's interesting that the people who complain about quotas are the people who lose the percentages.

ANDERSON: Of course. That's such an emotional issue right now and it's very difficult to figure out.

HOWELL: I think what scares people is the idea that there's a fixed number, and the number decides everything—which really isn't the point at all. The point is that the existing numbers are wrong.

ANDERSON: I'm sure it depends upon your point of view. But you do see what happens when you give people a chance. It's so inspiring. That's what I love about this women's group I now belong to—there are a lot of young women in it and when they first come, they're kind of shy, but then watching them learn to speak up is a thrill.

HOWELL: Earlier, you said that you had used gadgets as defense. Has that changed now, with your more political stance?

ANDERSON: That's a good question. I mean, I did it because it's magic. And I thought the whole last year [1991] was anti-magic.

HOWELL: This last show [*Voices from the Beyond*] is very stripped-down.

ANDERSON: And I really enjoyed it. I thought it would look really different if I stopped working with so much technology for a year; then I thought something very different would happen in the next big show. So, in *Halcion Days*, the images are in a different form, although it's still another magic show. I was getting really distraught over that for awhile, but I actually want to see a twelve-foot tornado enough to go to the trouble of building one and carting it around and going, "Look at this thing."

HOWELL: I suppose the reputation might be that these are things you place between yourself and an audience. Or it's easy to wow people with little symbols, like showing a clock to people who've never seen one.

ANDERSON: Yeah. And then you can talk about your own time-warped ideas to get people's attention. Maybe to push them into wondering, "How does that work? How does anything work?" It's like listening to the Dalai Lama teach. He'll say something really strange and you won't judge things the same way after that. Like his very disarming way of saying, "I don't know why I'm the Dalai Lama. Why should anyone be the Dalai Lama? I don't know. Should there be a Dalai Lama?" And then you go, "Yeah, maybe I'm the Dalai Lama." That's a possibility. It's to just open the door a little bit. And I guess I also used gadgets in that way as well— to show something magic and then hide behind it. Hiding and showing are very much the same for me, in a way. I'm not going to stand in front of this thing that I think is interesting enough to show to other people.

HOWELL: One of the beauties of being a performance artist in the early days was that it was just you and your stuff in a gallery for a night. Really simple. And the economics of it were simple, because they didn't exist. Somebody might have given you a hundred dollars or something.

ANDERSON: I might have made a hundred dollars but I'd spend [more than that doing it]. I remember once making a princely sum— eight hundred dollars—at the Museum of Contemporary Art in Chicago. They paid me to do *Songs and Stories for the Insomniac* or something like that. And I thought, "This is amazing. I'll be able to pay the air fare out of that. And we'll sleep at my parents' place." It would never have paid for the slides, but I brought two people, which was the most luxurious thing I could imagine.

HOWELL: How does your work finance now?

ANDERSON: By itself.

HOWELL: It makes that much money?

ANDERSON: Well, this work [*Halcion Days*] is a commission. It's sponsored by Expo and by two German theaters. For that wonderful privilege of being the commissioning theaters, they have to be listed as that, and that's it.

HOWELL: Do you make most of your money that way?

ANDERSON: I haven't made a record in three or four years. That's not unusual for me. I guess touring is the way I make about three-quarters of the money.

HOWELL: If you were starting out to be a performance artist now, could you do it the way you did then? How would you do it? Would you go the grant route?

ANDERSON: Oh, these poor artists without the NEA. It's going to be dead. Even Harvey Lichtenstein [*president and executive producer at BAM—JH*] said it'd be better not to have it. [*Lichtenstein later explained "I meant that if the NEA was so watered down to exclude controversial art, it might be better to have no NEA. I feel strongly about the integrity of the NEA, but I also feel strongly about keeping it alive. I would abandon the NEA only as a last resort."—JH*]

HOWELL: Do you remember your first grant?

ANDERSON: Yeah, New York State Council for the Arts.

HOWELL: How much was it?

ANDERSON: I think five hundred dollars. I was on the top of the world. Not so much because of the cash, although that was really important. It was that somebody said that my work was worth something.

HOWELL: It was valid enough for them to try to help you.

ANDERSON: Yes, that was really important to me. And I know it's that way for artists starting out now. That's why I'm doing all these things for the Endowment, like going on "Crossfire" and going to these press conferences. It's not so much because of all the support the NEA gives to the traditional arts here—which is important, it's preserving a heritage—but because of what it would mean for artists who are just starting out, to lose it. Whether you're working at a Xerox place or waitressing, you try to get ahead so that you can spend that money on your work. Artists are able to do some things without grants, but there are projects that they really want

Laurie Anderson gained her facility on the violin, playing in the Chicago Youth Symphony orchestra.

to do, and they can't quite get far enough ahead to pay for it.

HOWELL: I think fewer artists will do fewer things and with more difficulty. Art won't stop altogether.

ANDERSON: Of course, it won't stop. But the hoax of "corporate support" is absurd.

HOWELL: They're just dying to come and find you starting out in your career and help you out.

ANDERSON: They couldn't care less.

HOWELL: There was this brouhaha about the so-called "obscenity clause" and the issue of whether or not an artist should sign a grant contract if that clause is included. One attitude was that individual artists should sign it and take any money they can get, then proceed according to their own feelings anyhow, whereas more visible institutions with other sources of income should refuse money that comes with those clauses.

ANDERSON: Saying that individuals and groups should have different policies is difficult, because they're connected. And sometimes they're part of an NEA project without knowing it. One of the points I read in an editorial about Franklin Furnace was that the military requires discipline and art requires freedom. It's as simple as that. We have different requirements of different people and institutions. The National Endowment has a completely hands-off mandate, which has been agreed upon and signed. That's in the books. I just hope that Pat Buchanan paid the creators of *Tongues Untied* really well to use their tape for his ads; he can't legally do that for free, can he?

HOWELL: I don't think so. David Wojnarowicz [visual artist] got after Donald Wildmon [*an evangelist campaigning vigorously against "obscenity in the media"—JH*] for illegally duplicating his art without paying royalties.

ANDERSON: I hope he is getting great royalties.

HOWELL: When you were touring with *United States* in Europe, you often had mixed feelings. On one hand, you would tell me that Europeans responded more strongly to things you wished American audiences would respond to. But, on the other hand, you said, "It's a real burden that they take everything so seriously. I represent America and they want to believe the worst, so they love it when American artists come over and tell them how rotten and failed and corrupt America is." It is a complex relationship; you probably know as much about that as anybody.

ANDERSON: I became a patriot for that reason. It actually went full circle. I started writing it because I went to too many European dinner parties where they would say, "How can you live in a place like that?" That's an eight-hour answer. Then, when I presented it there, I became very defensive, saying, "It's not that bad." For example, the BBC was doing a show about the decline and fall of America and they were getting a lot of writers and artists to proclaim themselves on this. After an hour-long interview with them, I hadn't really said that I thought America was going down the tubes—which is what they wanted me to say. So they were basically asking, "Could you rephrase that?" And I said, "I'm absolutely not going to say that," and I became so much more enthusiastic about how well things are going in this country that I ended by saying, "It's such a great challenge now, and it's so interesting. It's at its turning point. Look at all the excitement and the people questioning things." After I finished the interview, I thought, "What did I just say?" I think the opposite, actually. I look around at this country and I'm completely disheartened. Both political parties have nothing for me. Neither of them even vaguely represents what I think this country should be. As the president of NOW says, "Fie on both of their houses!"

HOWELL: If you look at the principles on which the NEA was founded, they're quite idealistic—that's the America we want to believe in.

ANDERSON: I don't know if I think they're very idealistic. They are very Republican.

HOWELL: Well, the idea is that they're supposed to be hands-off.

ANDERSON: I'm thinking back to John Jay [*first Supreme Court justice—JH*], who said that those who own this country ought to judge it. That's how it was founded. White, male landowners. So it depends on which side of the flag you're trained to pull. It's a tug-of-war. I don't know really what it means, although I have a feeling that Americans are naive and generous and basically good people. Maybe not deep thinkers; I think we do stuff more than we think about it. And we're also a bit voyeuristic, so that when somebody

Americans love the law, and we love vicarious sex. So when those two are combined in sex trials, it's a kind of heaven for us.

like Pat Buchanan comes along, we're puritanical enough to go, "Yeah, that's really offensive." And, also, we love the law, and we love vicarious sex; when those two are combined in the sex trials, we're happy. This is like heaven for us, to be able to look into people's lives in a gossipy kind of way, but to have big federal laws apply to the situation. The ultimate thing—every woman's nightmare—is her underwear being sent to the FBI. Your little polka-dotted underwear or your pantyhose are being examined by the Supreme Court and you're going, "Is it really that interesting?"

HOWELL: I know people in Paris who rented hotel rooms to get access to the cable channels showing the Clarence Thomas hearing. Europe cannot begin to comprehend it. Even for Americans, it was a bit much.

ANDERSON: Our definition of the word "scandal" is really so different. They love to think we're puritanical twits, but I think they're jealous that we can just roll in this kind of stuff and watch it on TV while they're saying, "Oh, they're having so much gossipy, high-time fun." I really think they're jealous. They, of course, are used to a government official having three mistresses, and they think, "We're used to that because we're so sophisticated, and you Americans are just so silly about that kind of stuff."

HOWELL: Your work, whether it's an individual song or a whole performance, involves lots of parts. How do you put all that together?

ANDERSON: It's how you put it together that is the work of art. I put it together in a certain way, but I don't dictate whether you should be looking exactly there or hearing exactly that. As you look at it, you invent it yourself. It's open enough to do that. When I interviewed John Cage, one of my questions was, "Do you have a favorite work?" which is a way of saying one thing is better than another. The answer he gave was mystifying.

> *A song or story has to have three things: what you're saying, the color of the word, and the pace or tone.*

He said, "If it doesn't work, then there's something wrong with me, not with the work, because that's just the result of chance." But any time guilt is a part of an operation, I'm a little bit suspicious. Why would you blame yourself? You either can't see enough chaos or can't appreciate it. And anyway, what is chaos? When I think about how to finish a work and make it tight enough or loose enough, I always try to ask myself those questions. If a song or a story only

Electronically manipulated phone conversations frequent Anderson's pieces.

means one thing, and it's coded so exactly that you have to break it like a bad pun, that's not enough. It has to have three things, even if you're just dealing with language: There's what you're saying, the color of the word, and the pace or the tone. With language, you can open up a sentence so that it can be very free, open to interpretation. That's why I like language that's more conversational; thinking of it as a script flattens it out into something that doesn't have as many question marks hovering all over the place. That's the kind of language I like. When I have to perform in another language, it is like reading. It loses the texture, which is really important to me.

HOWELL: Do most of your songs start with the words or does the music come to you first? Or is it different for different songs?

ANDERSON: Different for different things. I have scrap notebooks with words, and then I have a lot of pulse things, and then I see which things would like to go together for the evening and if they're still together the next morning...

HOWELL: When you conceive of these things, I know it's you who puts them all together—you think of tornados, screens, words, music—but you always work with a herd of collaborators.

ANDERSON: They have no idea what I'm doing.

HOWELL: I think of them as your translators, realizing things you think of.

ANDERSON: An inventor from California designed a sort of electronic body-suit that I decided to use for my new show—he had only made a couple of them—and I am still trying to figure out what it can do in a performance. It's like when I sit for days sampling my collection of sound effects and watching the videos that I'm making at the same time—I just try to find something that resonates. I rummage through a bunch of stuff.

HOWELL: And some things are more interesting than others. Some conjunction resonates. What is that?

ANDERSON: It resonates at a different frequency, I'd have to say, to be really stupid about it. But it's true. If I'm working with a very light and sweet image, and I find some horrifying ominous sound and a very flatly delivered language thing, I'll try that out, but it may just be too much. I like it when you tend to wonder about what you're seeing and hearing.

HOWELL: It puts it slightly off-balance. I think of the audience sitting and watching one of your shows, and as it goes on, they just sort of tilt.

ANDERSON: Yeah, that's good. One side of their brain is getting heavier.

HOWELL: A door will be open and shut, but you don't hear it because you don't think it's important. Yet when you hear it amplified or brought to attention, you think, "Oh, that's what that thing sounds like." To me you bring a conjunction of those things that make people pay attention to something. There's always a tilt to it. What that does for people is a good question, I suppose.

ANDERSON: Hopefully it's freeing. I guess that's what I'm trying to do—free myself.

HOWELL: If it resonates for you, it might vibrate out there.

ANDERSON: I just hope I'm an average enough human being. And plenty of times, I'm the only one who thinks something is funny; everyone else is going, "Huh?" It doesn't remind them of their Uncle Fred and a sound he used to make. They don't even have an Uncle Fred.

HOWELL: Do you revise shows when things like that happen?

ANDERSON: Yes.

HOWELL: Things drop out?

ANDERSON: Yes. If I get enough blank stares, it's gone—I can entertain myself at home talking about Uncle Fred. I have all these stories I call "Osky stories." Osky is actually the name of a filter in one of my pieces of sound equipment. It makes me sound like the dorkiest person you could ever imagine, so I tell these stories about this character called Osky. I'm sure I'm the only person who would find this funny. I picture Osky being from Cream City, which is a place my father used to talk about. He and his friends used to go to Cream City and they would have all these adventures there. I don't even know if there is a Cream City. I picture him and maybe Osky going there. I've just really begun to appreciate my Dad, too. Because of who he is, which is a very slap-happy guy; you'll never meet a more typical Midwesterner. And he is very curious—still. He's eighty-one. I adore him so much, and always have. I see other old coots and I know how to talk to them. It's like a secret language he taught me, how to relate to a certain kind of salesman—I've got a pipeline right to their brains, and he gave it to me. I can understand [William S.] Burroughs in that same sort of way. Ron Delsener [concert promoter], same thing. It's like instant rapport. I finally met Ken Nordine [*a Midwestern radio announcer—JH*] a few months ago in Chicago. I called him up. Got his number—I've never done this before—and just said, "I love your work. I really think you're just wonderful. Could we meet?" And he said, "Sure, come on over."

HOWELL: Did he know who you were?

ANDERSON: Yes, he did. So I went over there and he's this enormous Swede. Really huge. Granddad. So jovial. His wife was making Swedish hard cookies. His son was working with him. He's got a great recording studio and a huge old house in downtown Chicago. He was so lovely, not at all like the paranoid guy I'd pictured. He was this expansive, funny, generous Swede who said, "I've got hockey tickets; I know all the politicos. Here. Have a couple." He gave me these hockey tickets and then I said, "If you ever want to do some Bible stories with me, I'd love to. Because that's what I'd really like to do. Re-write the Bible." So we have half a plan.

HOWELL: Do you think it's easier now to see where you come from, things like your parents?

ANDERSON: Yeah, I appreciate them more. Everybody does.

HOWELL: Do you see ways that you're more like them or things they taught you that you weren't even aware you were using?

ANDERSON: I used to resent the ways I was like them, of course. And now I actually realize how much they gave me and I truly appreciate it.

HOWELL: You mentioned your father, and Cage and Burroughs and Ken Nordine, who obviously had an influence on your work. They are roughly comparable, these old coot kind of guys.

ANDERSON: They have a wonderful curiosity and a very special sense of humor. And they are very modest and unassuming. Not at all egotistical—the opposite. They just want to see what's going on in this world, they've got their eyes open. But also there is this aspect of salesmanship which is really fascinating to me. Bullshitting.

HOWELL: Do you think of yourself that way?

ANDERSON: Sure. Bullshitting salesman. Absolutely. Sometimes it's exactly that, in some of the voice cartoons that I do.

HOWELL: I often thought people in New York weren't that familiar with people in other parts of the country, with that cartoonish

Anderson surrounded by keyboards, but always with a phone nearby.

quality that used to be thought of as quintessentially American. Optimism and relentless cheerfulness. Do you think New York audiences miss that completely or think you're making fun of it?

ANDERSON: The more I poke around, the more I find that cities really have personalities. That's what keeps me here: the mysterious quality of New York. When I go to Los Angeles, I feel that I'm in a city where people basically don't wish each other well. I don't feel that here. In Los Angeles, if you fail, there are people around who go, "Ha ha, you failed!"

HOWELL: "Now there's more room for me to succeed."

ANDERSON: Also, success is based on things like people saying, "I don't know I just have a feeling for a good story. I don't know how I got it. It's just in me." That is a very nebulous sort of skill.

HOWELL: Or success is whatever makes the most money.

ANDERSON: Yeah. If that's the basis of your success, it really could evaporate any second. You could just lose that nose, and then you don't even know how to use a word processor. You're up a creek then. And a lot of people in New York are finding that, too. Especially the people who lost their jobs after the big boom. They're really horrified. They made a huge amount of money and then suddenly lost their jobs; it's been three years and they haven't been able to find that job that makes three hundred thousand dollars a year, and they've spent all their money, and they're going to live with their parents.

HOWELL: Are there other major influences on what you do? When you started performing, were there people you gravitated toward or wanted to be like?

ANDERSON: Vito Acconci.

HOWELL: He'd come to your show and sit in the front row?

ANDERSON: No, I don't think he'd do that. But I would have loved it if he had. And, yeah, he has a starring role in this script that I wrote. Not that anything will ever happen to it. I want to pay him back someday.

HOWELL: What did he do for you?

ANDERSON: He made me laugh really a lot. He was so emotional. Nobody else was acting like that, and I thought, "Wow! A man being like that. That's incredible." And he was very funny at the same time. A great writer. That's what I really like a lot. He was and is a great poet. I love just listening to him speak. I really like guys with great voices. When I think about all these guys, they all have amazing, gravelly, deep, intoxicating voices. Burroughs. Cage. Cage has a softer version of it, but it's melodious in a special way. Vito, classic. Ken Nordine.

HOWELL: Can women have these voices?

ANDERSON: It's a different thing; it doesn't do the same thing to me. I wanted to ask women with voices to do things behind those blue dots that are used to hide defendant's faces on televised trials. So I asked Yoko Ono, classic. Karen Finley, Molissa Finley, Julia Heyward, Suzanne Vega. And while I love all their voices, it's more of a wailing thing or a Southern thing. You know, when anyone preaches it's got to be a Southern accent. It's hard for me to listen when Karen Finley starts talking Southern. I hunch down in my seat for some reason. Use your own voice, please. And while I love that way of speaking—of all these women I've mentioned—it doesn't do what the gravelly voices do to me. It's more of a saxophone. The women's voices are more waily and a little more hysterical and primal—which can make me shiver—but they're not so involved in narrative stuff that would just go on and on and unravel and unfold.

HOWELL: Do you have favorite writers? People who write in ways that you like, but that you don't necessarily hear yourself?

ANDERSON: I asked Cage that question: "When you read a book do you hear a voice?" And he said he hadn't thought about it, but he was going to think about it, so I'll ask him again. I just read Mark Helprin's *Winter's Tale*. That didn't have a voice. It's very written. Beautiful book. I really liked that so much. What I heard was branches, with ice frozen around them, clinking together—because he told you to hear that. And other than that, deep silence. It was a very telepathic sort of book. And really magic. Wasn't it great to read a book about New York that made it magic like that? The gleam faded from this place fifteen years ago.

HOWELL: Was it *Voices from the Beyond* where you went out at night and took pictures for some period of time?

ANDERSON: Oh, that was for *Empty Places*, and I did learn to love it [New York] better. *Winter's Tale* made me feel closer to it, just to have an image from a hundred years ago of the Hudson River being totally frozen, and people skating down from who-knows-where up in the mountains. You forget that the river really goes somewhere and that you're just living along it, and that New York City is not the end of the world.

HOWELL: Do you have favorite musicians?

ANDERSON: No. Well, Captain Beefheart, of course. Another gritty, growly guy. I'm a total sucker for them. And also anyone who could say, "Something-something-something in striped light. Pink flamingos in a food fight." Every time I really need to get cheered up, I try to imagine pink flamingos having a food fight and I'm right there. I can see that happening! I'm really grateful to him for having written those two lines, only one-and-a-half of which I can remember.

HOWELL: Somebody asked me once if you ever improvised and I said, "Not willingly."

ANDERSON: That's correct. Would you mind doing my interviews from now on?

HOWELL: How do you feel about hearing Laurie Anderson-type voices on television commercials? Has that appropriation happened more than once?

ANDERSON: Yes it has. Sometimes they just lift the whole song and put it in.

HOWELL: They can't do that.

ANDERSON: They can and they do.

HOWELL: They know how to get around it. They transpose.

ANDERSON: I got one card company on that, but it was difficult. You know, you call up and say, "I'm sorry, you've got my song, or at least it sounds exactly like it," and they go, "Oh, I guess you're right." The thing is, they hire production companies who either lift it off a record or sample it and redo it slightly. In the case of the card company, my lawyer said, "I think you should sue them," and I said, "That sounds horrible," and he said, "I'm going to threaten them with it." Then they said, "Well, you absolutely don't have a case to sue, but we are going to pay you an enormous amount of money because you shouldn't sue us. You don't have a case." And then I said, "No, I don't want the money." And they said, "Good, we'll do it." And I said, "No, I really don't want the money." And my lawyer said, "Okay, I'll tell them that." And they doubled it again. He was having a great time.

HOWELL: It always struck me as funny that you and Phil Glass were always placed by the mainstream world as experimental and avant-

Former Zappa traveller, Captain Beefheart.

garde, and then I hear you on commercials all the time.

ANDERSON: That's how it works. Where else are they going to get an idea? I know what these ad agency production houses are like. They have a whole bunch of records and they go, "Okay, we've got to sell cotton. What's a nice, soft, feminine thing?" They try the music out as a slug. Works pretty well. They maybe sample it and then redo it exactly as it is and give it to the company sponsoring the ad. The company doesn't know shit about the music, so they say, "Fine, sounds really nice," and never get any release. I didn't sue them, even though they had used my music exactly. At that point, I just told my lawyer to tell them to stop using it—and they did, actually.

I take from pop culture all the time; it's time they took something from me. But the main thing is, they have to ask me.

HOWELL: Why don't they call you up and say, "We'd like to use these?"

ANDERSON: Because I would say no.

HOWELL: Well, obviously, any artist doesn't like it.

ANDERSON: No, I think some people do appreciate being part of pop culture in that way. I mean, I was half-flattered, sure. I take from pop culture all the time. It's time they took something from me. But the main thing is to ask. It's not really fair to just take it. On the other hand, I've given my music to a lot of places. The German government hired an American ad agency—I think it was Young and Rubicam—for a campaign to convince neo-Nazi skinheads to stop torturing foreigners. It's been a huge problem there. The agency called me up in a huge panic saying, "We're using your music in this campaign and it's coming out in Germany tomorrow." And I said, "Wait a second, what's it for?" And they said, "It's a humanitarian thing. It's gonna be all over Germany. It's gonna be great." And I said, "I want to see a copy before you put it out. I may want to do it, but maybe I won't." And they said, "We'll send someone over right now with the three-quarter, on the next plane out, because it's going out tomorrow." And I said, "Don't spend any more money on this, guys. Play it this weekend. Send it to me special delivery now so I have it Monday. I'll look at it then and then we can make a decision." And it was actually a very good ad. There is also an AIDS ad that's been playing in

Italy for about three years. They did ask me in both of those cases. The AIDS people asked me six months in advance. Basically, if it's about selling stuff, they don't ask, and if it's about humanitarian stuff, they ask. I don't know what that means.

HOWELL: Do you consider yourself a successful artist? How do you even define success? Obviously you are successful to some extent, in that you are able to do your work the way you want to.

ANDERSON: Yes, that's an enormous privilege. To be able to wake up and ask, "What should I do today?" But there is also, obviously, a lot of anxiety attached to that. Like, what if I've just done my last work of art for the rest of my life? I'm going to be a lonely, isolated person with no pension. I have to keep producing—I don't have an employer.

HOWELL: Is that your biggest fear?

ANDERSON: My biggest fear is being isolated.

HOWELL: Isolated from your work, or isolated from within?

ANDERSON: No. My biggest fear is losing contact with other people, forgetting how to express things or just suddenly not being able to communicate at all.

HOWELL: Discovering that you're talking to yourself, maybe?

ANDERSON: Yes. That would be horrible, because then I would be doing pointless work. I believe you can do a masterpiece that way. I believe that someone alone in a room could make the world's finest painting but only that artist would know. I couldn't do that. I do sit around and laugh a lot when I'm working, though, and sometimes it's very entertaining. I can just look at something and I'll be on the floor in my studio by myself, just saying, "Yes! Yes! This is so funny!" I'll play it five hundred times in a row, laughing every single time. You'd think that would be reward enough, but nope, I have to get other people to laugh at it too. How greedy. But unless it makes that jump it's not finished for me. And I like to be there when it makes that jump. I like to be there to watch it happen. That's why I like doing live stuff.

HOWELL: So it would never be an option for you to just make videotapes or records and send them out without being there in person.

ANDERSON: That would feel cynical to me in some way. I know that's really judgmental, because plenty of people do that and it's really satisfying for them; they hate being in front of people. But for a hermit, I'm pretty social. I enjoy it.

HOWELL: I don't think of you as a hermit. Despite the image the sixties kids had, we work a lot. I think people looked at our generation and thought we were going to be the biggest fuck-off generation in America, that we were just going to grow up to smoke pot.

ANDERSON: That's true, and look what happened—we're a bunch of workaholics.

HOWELL: I guess we played just enough to get it out of our systems. My nephew is twenty-two, and he certainly hasn't had as much weirdness in his life as I'd had by the time I was his age. It's more like the fifties now—life's a bitch, then you die. You graduate into the worst job prospects in the history of America. They're all terrified about that.

ANDERSON: And terrified of sex.

HOWELL: Everything is a mortal threat to them, everything that's important. We had quite a different experience.

ANDERSON: I'm really grateful for that, aren't you? Ours is the right generation to be in.

HOWELL: It sure is—everyone else missed the party. Do you ever fear, though, that you'll just completely run out of ideas?

ANDERSON: Of course. I've been fearing that for twenty years.

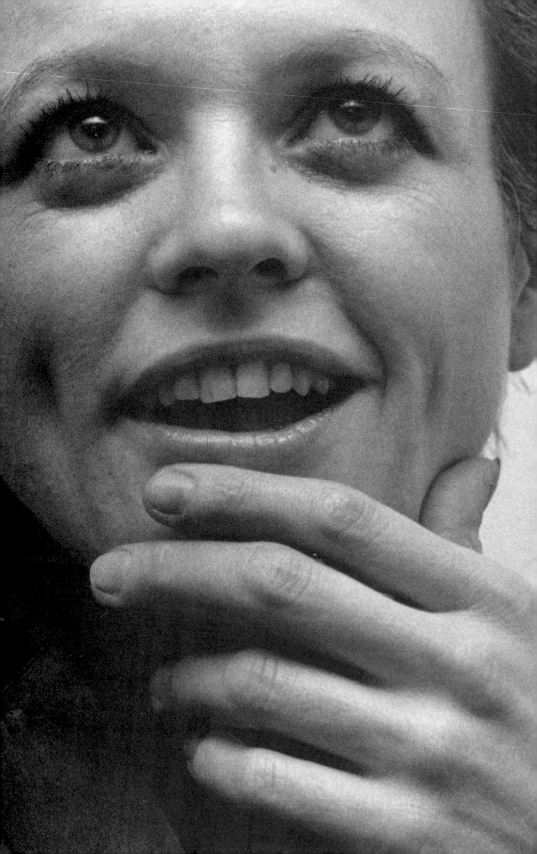

NEW RELEASE

DRAWINGS BY LAURIE ANDERSON

P. 106-107
From United States performance at the Brooklyn Academy of Music, 1983.

P. 108-119
Projected images from the film, Home of the Brave, 1986.

P. 120-121
From "Blue Lagoon", on the album United States, 1983.

P. 122-123
Storyboard from United States performance at the Brooklyn Academy of Music, 1983.

P. 124-125
Storyboard from United States performance at the Brooklyn Academy of Music, 1983.

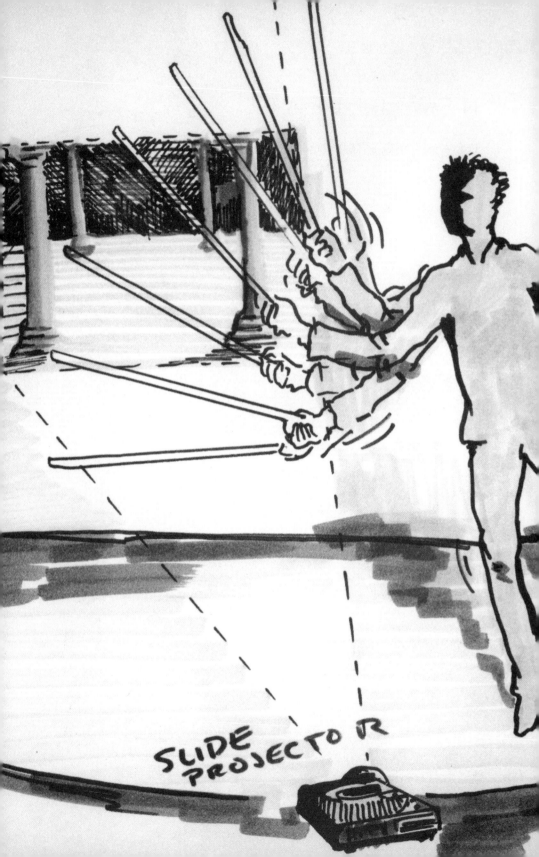

SLIDE
PROJECTOR

FROM 'PICTURES OF IT':

IMAGES OF A ROOM
ARE PROJECTED ONTO CEILING
[OUT OF SIGHT OF AUDIENCE]

WHITE VIOLIN BOW CUTS
INTO PLANE OF FOCUS,
CREATING A 'SCREEN.'

ROOM FLOATS MIDAIR.

Tuesday

had learned
_E in my sleep
all Peter
get more film!
design T-shirt's

— dark gray
"sweat marks"
SILK SCREEN †
SELL ON TOUR!

– should the un-born
rights ?
　YES. BECAUSE they
for it later.
– should the dead
　No. BECAUSE they

1. ca

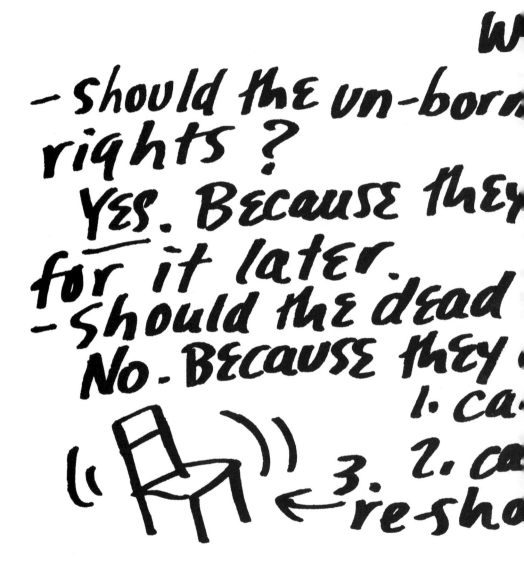

3. 2. ca
←re-sho

ONESDAY: PM
_____

have civil

can thank you

have civil rights?
an't talk anymore.
cel concert
1 Paula
t chair film

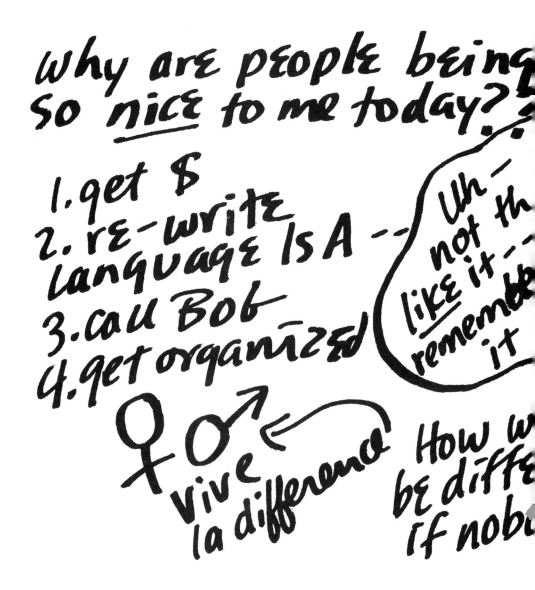

why are people being
so _nice_ to me today?

1. get $
2. re-write
   language Is A --
3. call Bob
4. get organized

Uh--
not th
like it --
remembe
it

vive
la difference

How w
be diffe
if nob

112

31'
Hamster

SP
Sl
Sr

←50'→

She was a cocktail wait
He was a N.Y. Jet --
Oooo... They were made fo
Unfortunately, they
never met....

"I'D T
BUT THERES
STUCK

Friday

d of Darkness :
ver or faster than
ed of light ??

ss — —

each other

YOU MORE
AN ICICLE
MY THROAT!"
— ANTONIN
ARTAUD

Brides? They should
mind 'their own busin
POSSIBLE PEACEFUL
WEAPONS RESEA

1. JUMP
START YOUR
PICK-UP
TRUCK FROM
OUTER SPACE

Ct

↱ AVERAGE BIRD

S /

Saturday

SES OF
H :
2. LIGHT YOUR GIRL
FRIEND'S CIGARETTES
BY LASERS
FROM
ORBITING
SPACE
STATIONS.

XCELLENT
RD

← PRETTY
AWFUL
BIRD

—turned a corner
in Soho today & s[
at ME & said:—

1. stop being
self-conscious
2. think TOTS

TALK NOR[

LIGHT BULB SWINGS

REAR PROJECTION SCREEN, 40' x 50'

LIGHT

ACCORDION

NEON VIOLIN

TA
BO
VI

OBXa

SYNCLAVIER

COMPUTER

SOPRANO

124

"THE SUN IS SHINING SLOWLY...."

125

Behind Anderson on the keyboards, multi-layered projections often include computerized visuals, text, slides and film.

LANGUAGE AND IMAGE, THEME AND MOTIF

BY JANET KARDON

I n dealing with Laurie Anderson's complex works, we encounter sets of themes, images and motifs. Like any body of data they can be categorized and cross-referenced to suggest ways of thinking about Anderson's visual/verbal habits.

Typography: Anderson's newsprint works, 1971-72, incorporated found texts; in 1972 her own compositions were often hand printed for a book or a slide format. Typewritten texts were inserted in the gallery objects of the late seventies, and in *United States* digital letters moved horizontally in both directions across a large screen. None of these type scripts has been abandoned, but they are added to previous styles.

Narration: Although Anderson's narration includes third-person parables as well as the earlier one-person reminiscences, conversational clichés remain the primary framework in the stories and the songs, interspersed with fifties jargon, slang and the conventions of late-forties film-noir scripts. Anderson witnesses a culture through its vernacular language patterns or personal trivia. Like Woody Allen, she can deftly turn the trivial and ordinary into serio-comic discourse.

A rear screen projection, with Anderson silhouetted, from Home of the Brave, 1985.

Sign Systems: In addition to texts, she relies on several images, which represent a discrete Anderson iconography—clocks, maps, charts, grids and ideogrammatic line drawings, all devices for either organizing or transmitting information. Of all of these, the clocks seem to be most important in Anderson's medium of performance. One of the early performances, appropriately housed at the Clocktower [*an alternative arts center in New York—JH*], was titled *In the Nick of Time,* in which she played her violin, told her family stories, and recounted her dreams. Clocks and calendars are prominent props in the *Dearreader* film, and images of the clock permeate *United States.* One of the stories in *Like A Stream,* 1978, reads, "His house was full of clocks. Clocks of all kinds. He was very particular about setting them so that they all told exactly the same time. But not only the same time . . . he set them so that they all ticked on exactly the same beat. So his whole house sounded like, 'TICK . . . . . TICK . . . . . TICK!!'"

Metronome: The metronome, a device for keeping time, has been part of Anderson's lexicon of images from the beginning, as well as a windshield wiper and other movements, which she uses as similes. The metronome was first seen in *Songs and Stories for the Insomniac,* performed at Artists' Space in 1975. In one reappearing stage gesture she waves her violin bow back and forth in an arc; sometimes the violin bow is lined with neon, creating an arc of light. These gestures, accompanied by the sound of drumbeats or by using her head as a percussion instrument insert the regularity of clock time in what otherwise appears to be a chaotic accumulation of isolated moments.

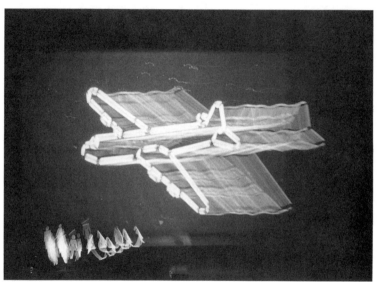

Anderson may be drawing on her own traumatic flying experience, when she refers to flight in both visuals and narration.

Flight: In Anderson's work the airplane appears as image, as acoustical element, and as the set for narratives. In one image, a vortex of cartoon-style planes move in circular patterns. The sound of planes is often inserted into her soundtrack, stories of flight appear more than once in the repertory, and aerial views are included in her image bank. When the narrative concerns flying, it is as though the passenger is being rushed on by an unstoppable process, urged on by the impersonal flight attendant's preprogrammed message, the habitual flight directions becoming absurd commentary.

Water: The Hudson River, seen from her loft window, is frequently used, as are other references to water. In *As:If,* a 1974 performance at Artists' Space, the metaphorical implication of the colon in the title was enlisted by projecting pairs of words—one word having to do with language and the other with water (for example, "sound:drown")—or an image of water with a word relating to it. In this piece she also filled her violin with water and it "wept" as she played a Tchaikovsky violin concerto. *Duets on Ice* concluded when the blocks of ice on which she stood melted into water.

Grid: Certain recurrent motifs in Anderson's work, such as the grid, are directly derived from a painter's or sculptor's vocabulary. "And that grid returns, flowing down the screen like a wave breaking, less like an Agnes Martin [painting] than a sheet of graph paper, maintaining a tight grip on nothing at all, dramatizing emptiness, a cipher denoting absence of language," (art critic Stuart Morgan).

Hands: Anderson's silhouetted hands might become a quacking duck or, as "seer," point the way. "If you can't way it, point to it" is one significant phrase. Eight white-gloved hands protrude from her body in a scene in *United States.*

Eyes: It is almost a photographic cliché to draw attention to the eyes as a symbol for the camera lens, and as a visual artist it is perhaps equally worn. Anderson uses phrases in songs like, "I no longer love your eyes" or in texts, "Your eyes . . . it's a day's work just looking into them," to quote the style of pulp novels or films. In another clichéd message, she refers to an automobile's headlights as its "eyes."

A home, with window, from Home of the Brave, 1985.

Light: In Anderson's work light becomes an almost palpable medium, carefully measured or sparingly allocated. The light from a projector might erase texts, silhouette the artist or be the stage light. The subdued light used in *Dark Dogs, American Dreams* imparted the aura of deities to photographic portraits of ordinary people. Only when the spectator blacked out the light in *Quartet #1 for Four (Subsequent) Listeners* could the messages be received. One needs darkness to view slides or film, and Anderson's stage wattage resembles that of the movie theater.

Windows: Window images with light pouring from them are effective devices on a darkened stage. Windows were a metaphor for paintings, especially in the nineteenth century; Anderson also refers in an early text to Vermeer, who exploited the window as formal element and as symbol. Anderson shoots many stills and film sequences through her loft window.

© F-STOP FITZGERALD

Holding a neon violin bow, Anderson is silhouetted by nuclear clouds.

The Movies: Juke Box and *Dearreader* both appropriate film conventions. When Anderson talks about a thirty-foot-high dog in a story, she refers to the alteration of scale that a movie imparts, where a dog that size is "real," as are babies the size of grownups. In one discussion, Anderson expressed a preference for the enormous images of the screen to television's "puny" images, and described film as "specks of light that are shimmering, scintillating and alive."

Memory: Time can only be retrieved through memory, which was one of the main themes of visual art in the mid-seventies. Anderson constantly recycles her own material, reusing her own past and history in creating new work. Thus her own memory is perhaps her most valuable resource. At first it was quoted directly, but now she is adept at altering or imitating the process of remembering. Anderson uses memory to blur the distinction between the past and the present and solidify the ephemerality of the moment.

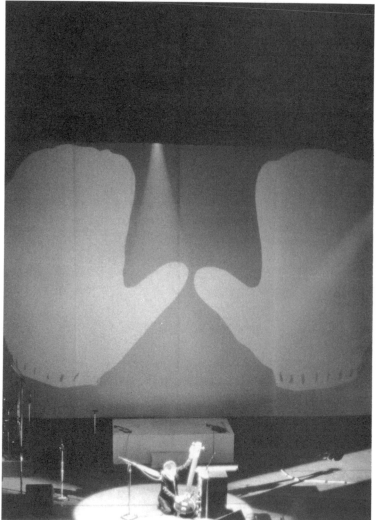

Anderson's formal training in classical music has stood her well, in her explorations as a performance artist. Here, she plays a sitar.

It is when the thematic content is considered that Anderson's diversity begins to fall along a single axis. Through all her apparent wanderings, willful hesitations, rehearsals and re-presentations we are aware of a mind that tracks itself from its earliest manifestations with a single-minded force. Her method of attack—oblique, brightly sinister—is in a tradition of American humor that encompasses both the whimsy of Stephen Leacock and S.J. Perelman, and a darker humor that plays up the absurdity of everyday life. The key to Anderson's art is truly, as she claims, language. The duplicity of the voice cannot be avoided as it re-peoples an absent self or, more accurately, a self that is tuned down to almost zero. This is supported through bits of electronic magic and visuals she uses to surround not so much her figure as her voice.

Far from being incomprehensible, Anderson's art occupies several familiar territories that were carved out by certain New York avant-gardes over the past thirty-five years. Her art works brilliantly within the conventions of juxtaposition and non-sequitur that replaced the exhausted surrealism of the late fifties and early sixties, (a surrealism that MTV has revived). These conventions run through large swathes of New York culture: Robert Rauschenberg in visual art, William S. Burroughs in literature, Merce Cunningham in dance, Richard Foreman in theater, perhaps John Cage in music. These figures have, I think, established the ground out of which Anderson, a member of a new generation, works with ease and aplomb, carefully organizing and orchestrating the random in a way that denies method even as it invokes it.

The germ of all this is present even in the earliest of her conceptual works where if there is an image and text, there is also a *frisson* between depiction and a voice. In classic conceptualism the reciprocal captioning of voice and image becomes the content; the work exists in the mutual interplay of illumination and counter-illumination. And in Anderson's work parallel streams of sound, image, voice and gesture leave sufficient gaps for free audience interpretation. Again, as in classic fifties and sixties avant-garde practice, the audience's ingenuity is tested; the most ingenious and educated "get the most out of it." If these streams of what we used to call "information" leave horizontal "gaps," the work is also interrupted by vertical "gaps," like the pregnant black-outs that separated the seventy-eight segments of *United States*. These vertical voids intersect the horizontal "gaps" to make up a kind of grid of nothingness which bears her work along, while paradoxically "fixing" its basic structure.

If we can call this structure the latent content, the manifest content offers a world view that is not unfamiliar. The point of entry—laconic observation—triggers an absurdity, maybe a neurotic fear, sometimes a witty parody of experience (in which an illogical premise is logically followed). This frequently leads to sets of word-plays, narrations and eccentric sounds that are never too far from describing an apocalypse that has become all too familiar, that has perhaps been this generation's unsung anthem of anxiety.

It is a world of the defenseless self, indeed of the disembodied self searching for a place in a placeless universe; encountering the opaque codes of the cynical "they": the generators of the anonymous language (advertising, commercials, instructions, the official, posted dos and don'ts of everyday life) that is appropriated unconsciously in our fantasies and dreams. Once again, in Anderson's world we come, as in classic Pop Art, to the terror, banality and awe of the capitalist Word. Anderson has monumentalized the Word by extending and shifting the time in which the Word appears, carefully bringing it into a structure that is built architecturally—but which exists episode by episode—to exhibit chaos and discontinuity.

This essay is reprinted with the permission of its author and the Institute of Contemporary Art, University of Pennsylvania, which published it in somewhat different form in the catalogue Laurie Anderson: Works from 1969 to 1983.

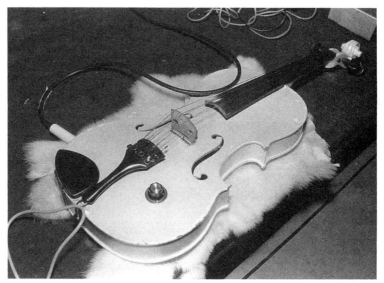

Anderson's signature white violin, cradled on a fur mat, before a performance of Americans on the Move, at the Market Street Cinema, San Francisco.

TIMELINE

Education

Bachelor of Arts, Barnard College, New York
Magna cum laude with honors in Art History
Phi Beta Kappa

Master of Fine Arts, Columbia University, New York
Sculpture

HONORARY DOCTORATE DEGREES

Art Institute of Chicago
San Francisco Art Institute
Philadelphia College of Art

Discography

1977-79   Various releases on 110 Records, Giorno Poetry
Systems, 1750 Arch Street Records, Holly Solomon Gallery

1981   *O Superman*, 7" EP, 110 Records/Warner Brothers Records

1982   *Big Science*, Warner Brothers Records

1984   *Mister Heartbreak*, Warner Brothers Records

          United States, 5-record set, Warner Brothers

1986   *Home of the Brave*, Warner Brothers Records

1989   *Strange Angels*, Warner Brothers Records

Filmography

1974   *Dearreader*

1979   *Fourteen Americans*

1981   *Film du Silence*

1986   *Home of the Brave*

1987   *Swimming to Cambodia,* soundtrack

1991   *Monster in a Box,* soundtrack

Videography

1982   *O Superman*, Warner Brothers

1984   *Sharkey's Day*, Warner Brothers

1985   *This Is the Picture*, with Peter Gabriel

1986   *Language Is a Virus*, Warner Brothers

1986   *What You Mean We?*, PBS

1986   *Alive from Off Center*, PBS

1989   *Talk Normal*, Pioneer Laser Disc Corporation

1990   *Beautiful Red Dress*, Warner Brothers

1991   *The Collected Videos*, Warner Brothers Home Video

1971   *The Package: A Mystery*, Bobbs-Merrill Co.

1974   *Transportation*, Laurie Anderson

1977   *Notebook*, Wittenborn Art Books

1979   *Words in Reverse*, Hallwalls (Buffalo, New York)

1984   *United States*, Harper & Row

1986   *Home of the Brave*, Talk Normal Productions

1990   *Postcard Book*, Canal Street Communications

1991   *Empty Places*, Harper Collins

A simple, backlit timpani drum-player swells to many times actual size, enhancing the bigger-than-life scope of Anderson's performing universe.

1979　　*Like a Stream*, for Oakland Youth Symphony,
　　　　Oakland, California

1982　　*It's Cold Outside*, performed in New York by American
　　　　Composers Orchestra, Dennis Russell Davies conducting,
　　　　and in Köln, Germany.

1984　　*Set and Reset*, collaboration with Trisha
　　　　Brown and Robert Rauschenberg

1986　　*Kyogen*, Robert Wilson performance

Performances (Selected)

1972   *Automotive*, Town Green (Rochester, Vermont);
Duets on Ice, New York and Genoa, Italy

1975   *As:If,* Artists' Space, New York; various pieces at the
Whitney Museum of American Art (Downtown Branch,
New York), Oberlin College (Oberlin, Ohio), Holly
Solomon Gallery (New York).

1976   Various pieces (including *For Instants, For Instants,*
Parts II and III, and *Engli-SH*)at the Museum of Modern
Art (New York), the Whitney Museum of American Art
(New York), Philadelphia College of Art (Philadelphia,
Pennsylvania), Akademie der Kunst (Berlin, Germany),
and the University of California (San Diego, California).

1977   Various pieces (including *Songs for Lines/Songs for Waves,*
That's Not The Way I Heard It, and *Some Songs*) at
the Kitchen (New York), Biennale (Paris, France), and
the International Cultural Center (Antwerp, Belgium).

1978   Various pieces (including *Like a Stream* and *Americans on*
the Move) at Walker Arts Center (Minneapolis,
Minnesota), Texas Opry House (with Contemporary Art
Museum, Houston, Texas), Contemporary Art Center
(Cincinnati, Ohio), and Het Tweed International Dichters
Festival (Rotterdam, Holland).

1979   Various pieces (including *Suspended Sentences,* and
Americans on the Move, Parts I and II) at Carnegie Recital
Hall (New York), Theater of Nations Festival (Hamburg,
Germany), Aspen Center for the Visual Arts (Aspen,
Colorado).

1980-83   Numerous performances (including various parts of
United States) in the United States and abroad (major
theaters, galleries and performances spaces).

1983   *United States, Parts I-IV*, premiere, Brooklyn Academy of Music (New York)

1984   *Mister Heartbreak* tour

1986   *Natural History* tour (United States, Japan, Australia, Spain, France, England, Germany, Sweden, Denmark, Switzerland, Italy)

1987-88   *Talk Normal* tour (United States, Europe, Asia)

1989   *Empty Places* premiere, Spoleto Festival (Charleston, South Carolina) and Brooklyn Academy of Music (New York)

1990   *Empty Places* tour (United States, England, Germany, Italy, Spain, Brazil, Argentina, Belgium, Sweden, Norway, France, Yugoslavia, Czechoslovakia, Hungary, Greece, Holland)

1991   *Voices from the Beyond* tour (United States)

1992   *Halcion Days: Stories from the Nerve Bible* (Spain, Germany)

Grants and Awards

1974	New York State Council on the Arts
1974-75	National Endowment for the Arts
1975	ZBS Foundation
1976	Gallery Association of New York
1977	New York State Council on the Arts
1977	National Endowment for the Arts
1979	National Endowment for the Arts
1981	Villager Award
1982	Guggenheim Fellowship